WHEN GOD BOWLS A GOOGLY

Other titles by Sri M

- The Little Guide to Greater Glory and a Happier Life
- Wisdom of the Rishis
  Ishavasya, Kena & Mandukya
- Jewel in the Lotus
  Deeper Aspects of Hinduism
- How to Levitate and other Great Secrets of Magic
  by James Talbot (Sri M)
- The Upanishads
  Katha, Prashna & Mundaka
- Shunya: *A Novel*
- On Meditation:
  Finding Infinite Bliss and Power Within
- Apprenticed to a Himalayan Master
  A Yogi's Autobiography
- The Journey Continues
  Sequel to Apprenticed to a Himalayan Master
- The Homecoming and Other Stories
- The Friend
  Mind, Body, Soul, Well Being
- Yoga Also For The Godless
- Kailash Yatra
  The Journey and Satsang with Sri M

To buy books and Digital downloads online visit
www.magentapress.in

WHEN GOD
BOWLS A GOOGLY

Ashwath Aiyappa

Magenta Press

ISBN: 978-93-82585-14-5
First printed January 2015
Second Printed December 2023

Cover design: Sonali Dhruve

Book design: J. Menon. www.grantha.com

Published by: Magenta Press and Publication Pvt. Ltd.,
33/5 2nd Floor Mount Kailash Building, Meanee Avenue Road Ulsoor
Bengaluru 560042 Landmark : Next to Lakeside Hospital & Above HDFC Bank
Contact: 91 6363083590 www.magentapress.in

Dedication

This book is dedicated to

My Ma and Papa

Thanks for all the security, stability, unconditional love and freedom that you have given me. I hope I can use all that for good, and sorry for all the times that I have caused you'll trouble, and sorry in advance for all the pain I may cause in the future. They say the soul chooses the womb ideally suited for its cleansing. It is pure grace and only grace that it chose you'll.

and

My late grandfather, Mr I I Kuttappa

A man of modest taste and thought, he believed in the adage "Work is Worship." His strength was his simplicity. He worked for a lifetime to secure the future of our families for generations to come. Yet, he had told me months before his passing, "Son, money cannot buy happiness." Clichéd though the saying may appear, I knew he had fully grasped its wisdom.

To Sri M, from the author

In him I see all my highest ideals fully realised. He is utterly fearless, completely free of hatred and full of unconditional love. The kind that most people think is impossible and therefore non-existent in today's commercial environment. I want to share a small story to explain why I say this. In 2011, at the age of 64, he was brutally attacked and the assailants nearly killed him. He received a severe thrashing and needed over 10 hours of surgery to recover. In the aftermath of the attack, not only was his recovery phenomenal, but more importantly I never saw him exhibit any trace of post-traumatic stress, despite being the target of some very dangerous men.

In an address shortly afterwards, he reassured everyone calmly saying, "An attempt has been made to derail my work, but don't worry it will go on." He added, "Nikal padenge khuli sadak par, aisa seena taan ke," meaning, "I will walk into the open streets, with my chest pushed out boldly." He also refused to let anybody publicise the incident and did not care whether or not the culprits were brought to justice. He nursed no grudge.

He went about his life as though nothing had happened. He refused the security cover and other paraphernalia that was offered to him, and did not cancel a single scheduled program. He continued to freely share his address and whereabouts with anyone who sought the information.

Of what metal is such a man carved? While this book deals with overcoming relatively selfish and petty psychological fears and pressures, here is someone, who according to me has conquered all fear, including the big one – death. After observing these traits I often ask myself, what experience has made him so daring? What knowledge has made him so kind? What realisation has made him so free? I simply don't know.

Is he willing to share his secrets? Of course he is, but are there enough takers? I should certainly think so, as crowds throng him and forever want to be by his side. But again I am not so sure, for he once said in a resigned tone, "My plate is full but nobody is hungry." So far to me Sri M is a bit of a Mystery.

It is my luck that I have been exposed to his rendering of our age-old wisdom, adapted practically to suit our time. And whatever I have understood of it has without a doubt made me a happier human being.

I simply want to say a heartfelt, Thank you Sir.

Contents

Acknowledgements

This will probably be my only book, so I thank everybody who has helped it happen starting with:

My Family
A heartfelt thanks to Amma, my brother, cousins and my entire extended family on either side.

Rahul Dravid
He is a towering figure of not just Indian cricket but world cricket. His encouragement and support were a huge confidence boost to me. A deeply felt Thank You, Rahul Sir.

My Impact Coaches
Starting with Shankar Swami, Mr Jaffer (Lawrence School, Lovedale), Mr Irfan, Mr Vijay Dhruve, Mr Pradeep Godbole, Mr Kinjal Suratwala, Mr Abey Kuruvilla, Mr Vijay Patil, Mr Shiraguppi, Mr Makarand Waingankar.

Also thank you to all the coaches at BPCA (Mr Suri, Mr Raghuram Bhatt, Mr Brijesh Patel and Mr Jaswanth), KIOC and Jawahars (Mr Prashant and Mr Basavaraj).

The world remains sane because of people like you'll. Take a bow.

My Editors
A very special thanks to my beloved editors Chetan and Ambika for both provoking and supporting me enough to finish this book.

My Chanakya
Thank you Raj Sir for bringing perspective, intelligence, objectivity, direction, routine and emotional support in trying times.

My Sporting Colleagues
Udit Patel, Abhishek Jagan, Sudhir Rao, Gopalan Bharadwaj, Niduvan G, K B Pawan, Aditya Sagar, Rohit, Arjun Gautam, Nitesh and Abrar Kazi.

Thanks for the many open spirited exchanges and support that took the burden away and made life so much easier to live.

Above all thanks for playing the game with your hearts on your sleeves.

Thanks also to
Sujith Somasundar, C B Karthick, S N Amith, Abhinav, Jonathan, Sudin, Kumar Subramanium, Ashok Kadam, Azar, Pravin Tambe, Yogesh Pawar, Kshemal, Balu, Raje, Paul V, H Bachani, Bunty Kambli, Ramesh Uncle and all those I played alongside at Karnataka and Mumbai.

My Off-the-field Special Friends
My cherished late friend Vipin Medappa aka 'Dappa' – it's been over 10 years since the Almighty snatched you away, I still miss you.

Thanks also to Oliver, Vasini, Viraj, Vrinda, Chumar alias Bobby, Manoj Dhanapal, Sheena Pinto, Nandan Rajeev, Padmini, Sonam, Arnav, Hari, Sandhya Rasiquina, Karan Asrani, Manoj Uthappa, Eva, Suzna, Vibha and Suri Uncle.

The Dhruves
Chetan, Sony aunty, Arjun, Vijay Sir, Rita bhabhi & family. Thank you guys for all the love and 'fud.'

And finally and most importantly,

Sri M
Thank you for bowling the 'Googly' so well and rescuing me from being consumed by my own demons. You make spirituality so 'cool.' Thank you Sir for being born.

Foreword

As a former sportsman who has represented India at the highest level, I would say that sport is particularly brutal on dreams. In the case of India and cricket, where the sport is a religion, there are many kids whose parents and coaches are pushing them extremely hard. Often, it goes well beyond pushing – children are forced to the extent that they are playing for others, not for the joy of playing.

In a nation as large and populous as ours, the odds are stacked against anyone wishing to play at the elite level. At any given time, only 11 people are playing for our country, 11 for your state, and 11 for your IPL team. If you're a batsman or bowler, those numbers reduce to four or five per team. If you're a wicketkeeper, that number is one.

Given that there are millions of youngsters with starry eyes, competition levels are fierce. These kids play through cold, heat, rain, and even physical pain. They travel on cycles, on foot or in crowded train compartments, just to get a shot at glory. Name and fame being their only definition of glory, they give up everything including education to pursue cricket, which is an extremely dangerous trend. In such intense environments, uncertainties and uncontrollables are enormous. Ignorance of this aspect can have grave consequences, while recognition of it leads to a balance in one's approach.

In contrast to many sportspeople, Ashwath though cricket obsessed, fortunately had the discipline to complete his Bachelor's degree in Computer Science. He co-founded and helped run a software company for over three years, which he then quit at age 26 to further pursue cricket. The point is that he developed other skills on the side to fall back on. I know a lot of players who do not give themselves that option; they are not interested in developing other marketable skills.

Money, fame, honour, talent and ambition make for a heady combination. Yet injuries, politics, family circumstances and a host of other factors can shatter the best laid plans. Unfortunately, the world is littered with the careers of famous sportspeople who lost their way despite high levels of achievement. Their stories are real eye openers.

I have had several roles – that of a player, selector, administrator and coach – for multiple age groups. I can tell you from experience that it is never easy to be the one to tell a youngster that he should quit, or break the news to parents that their child isn't gifted enough to play in the big league.

Mostly, this message is sent through a sterile and curt note in the form of a selection sheet, which informs a player whether or not he has been selected. This has vast emotional repercussions on players, which they are left to themselves to handle. As administrators, we do want to help as we understand the trauma. However, it is not humanly possible for us to counsel every single player.

The real question is, why is it so hard to tell the truth to someone? It's hard because we treat so-called failure as a disaster, as though there are no other avenues in life for happiness. Sporting success is pursued with single-minded fanaticism to the exclusion of family, friends, hobbies and other interests. This one-dimensional approach creates problems that can end in disaster if not dealt with maturely and carefully.

The plagues of gambling, betting and match fixing have lured many high profile and wealthy players, smashing our perceptions of these gifted individuals as mentally and morally tough. Not only are these players tainted forever, they are bad role models in a culture obsessed with celebrity. Their lives prove that natural ability isn't always enough. There is need for well-rounded development of the mind, as this will only better one's performance on and off the field as well.

This is where the book shines a light. I have known Ashwath and closely observed him for eight years during his time as a front-line batsman/keeper at the DY Patil Club. A complete team man, he was an integral part of three championship victories in five years. He has gone from being a Ranji probable at age 19 (for Karnataka) to a struggling cricketer at the fringes through his twenties, who never quite made the leap into the big leagues.

I have seen him succeed in extremely difficult matches – be it an unbeaten century in challenging conditions against a good BPCL (Bharat Petroleum) attack, a championship-winning 63 with a severely sprained ankle or pulling off one of the most stunning catches I have ever seen under pressure. I have also seen the same person succumb to the same pressures. He has dropped sitters as a wicketkeeper and thrown away his wicket at times.

I would be very frustrated with this dichotomy because the boy had the talent, intense desire, and commitment to succeed. It seemed sometimes like he was near, yet so far and this is true of many sportspeople. Something was amiss and Ashwath explains what that is, in this engaging portrayal of his journey.

The difference between mega success and not making it is minute and often depends on sheer luck. And whether or not you make it in your chosen sport, it's more important to be a well-adjusted and happy human being, which is where mental health plays a critical role. It is increasingly recognised that without this important facet of health, true success is impossible.

The field of sports psychology is usually taken to be a remedy for the emotional upheavals that accompany the vagaries of sporting life. Truth be told – sports psychologists are hired to teach teams how to win. No sports team hires a sports psychologist to lose. But we have enough sports psychologists. What we need is for someone to elucidate a process that helps us live emotionally healthy lives, particularly in the context of sport.

Increasingly, non-cricket sports such as shooting, hockey, football, tennis and badminton are also attracting attention. As these sports attract more and more people, the players could fall prey to the same pressures that cricketers do.

Through this book, Ashwath maps out the emotional journey of a sportsperson. He provides perspectives and insights, and makes one completely aware of potential pitfalls as well as solutions. He has committed two years to this book and has deeply explored the subjects he has written about. He intimately understands the mental states that bring about both success and failure.

I strongly recommend this book not just to youngsters and their parents, but also to coaches, critics, team owners, media, and sports teachers, because it's one of the first attempts at giving a closer view of the other side of success, which evidently is not so bad.

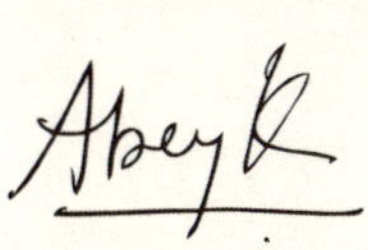

Abey Kuruvilla

- Former Test and One-Day International player, India
- Mumbai and India Under-19 selector
- Sports Director and Coach, DY Patil Sports Academy, Mumbai

Falling apart

THE CLOCK seemed to tick faster than normal, gobbling up time. I had covered seven of the 11 chapters required for my 2nd PUC board (math) exam. There were four topics left and 12 hours to do it in. "Game on!" I first thought.

Out of nowhere, I felt a sudden flood of thoughts overpowering the initial positive assertion. "What if I'm unable to finish the remaining chapters in time?" I asked myself. The reply I got was hardly reassuring: "Failure is not an option. Finish them or die" – my mind issued an ultimatum. I began seriously entertaining thoughts of doom; I suddenly became anxious about failing and its aftermath.

My young and inexperienced mind didn't know how to handle this threat. It simply set into motion a flow of terrifying thoughts that snowballed as I froze into inaction. The hostile-thought-torture seemed impossible to stem. I wished I could turn off my mind and even tried to drown my anxiety by eating and scribbling random figures onto a pad, forcefully attempting to distract those thoughts to oblivion. Nothing worked.

I believed I was already a failure for having such thoughts. Tears poured forth. "This is enough," I finally said to myself, desperately seeking to flee to a safe place free from the pain and pressure. I didn't want to be present when news of my failure reached everyone and I didn't want to say that I wasn't good enough. That mode of thought was opposite to the way I set myself up in my social environment.

I am a Kodava from Kodagu (Coorg) in Karnataka, and belong to a closely-knit middle / upper middle class family. I had just moved to Bengaluru and failure was simply not an option, that too when failing meant getting less than 80%. I had most of the portions covered yet I felt like I had not done enough. Under all this pressure and at a critical time, my mind was folding. It was the one time I wished I were a smoker or a drinker, so I could have just drowned or puffed away my sorrows.

One understands extreme suffering, strife or depression due to penury, oppression, war and pestilence. Mental and physical trauma on these counts is perfectly justifiable. But what of my exam kind of misery?

There was no poverty, I was materially comfortable, perfectly healthy, there was no war or famine, neither was anybody near nor dear dying. I was simply sitting for an exam and yet the psychological pain and desperation I experienced was as intense as any.

I got through that episode, thankfully, but all that drama got me ill. I was hospitalised and missed the exam. I wrote the paper later the same year and scored 86%, so that ended well. But I paid a big price for it cricket-wise. I lost two crucial seasons of development as a player, one season in exam preparation, and another for writing the exam as my parents took me back to Kodagu to prepare. All this meant I lost the momentum I had built up on the cricketing front, a year after I represented the state at the Under-16 level, at that time a proud achievement for a boy from Kodagu.

The pressure of performance that a professional cricketer faces day in and day out is often similar to a board exam. I am not ashamed now to admit that many a time I have felt as jittery, if not worse, when I have walked out into the middle to face a bowler or to keep wickets. I repeated mistakes several times over, and was unable for the longest time to free myself from the grip of my mind's emotional and mental programs, no matter how hard I tried.

I have deliberately chosen the exam incident, as it was the first time I felt so helpless and confused. Also, most people have experienced the fear of exams and can relate to it. Such fear, be it on account of a match or exam, may vary in form but not in character because of the harmful mental states it induces.

After the board exam episode, I began a search for answers because if it could happen during an exam, it could happen during a match or any similar situation. I knew a lot had to be fixed in my head. I was burning to know what causes one to feel so low and powerless. I never wanted to feel that way again. I wanted to be mentally impenetrable. I had several questions, some of which I've listed below:

- Why was the nature of my thoughts so negative or evil?
- How did my mind become like this?
- Why did I feel so much pressure?
- Why was my response so poor?

After long periods of trial and error, I found answers whose veracity was tested in a match against Western Railway. I scored an unbeaten century (113*) at the D Y Patil International Stadium in Navi Mumbai, at a time when my team needed it. I *finally understood that 99% of all these fears are purely psychological* and don't have their basis in fact.

On that day, I prevailed over age-old patterns that had taken root in my mind. It was also my 26th birthday – a good nine years since I had first started my search for answers. Like I said, it took me a while to arrive at them. And as the writer Zora Neale Hurston once said, "There are years that ask questions and years that answer." And it did take me years to understand how my mind gravitated towards a certain archetypal way of thinking.

I have spoken to many cricketers and coaches on these issues and found my experience to be in no way unique, as I once thought it to be. The difference is that some players pass off the experience as 'exam jitters' or 'pre-match jitters,' and don't go beyond the phrase. But for some, the intense pressure proves fatal to their careers and sometimes even lives.

Looking back at the exam incident, yes, I covered my pain and escaped from the situation by deliberately falling ill. But I now forgive myself. Society today is so designed that our complex and competitive personalities are set up or arranged around ideas that shiver at the very mention of disappointment and failure.

Setbacks are inevitable. When we understand this to be a natural phenomenon and reconcile ourselves to this fact, we develop a more accepting attitude towards so-called 'negative outcomes,' which truly are our most important teachers.

When you realise this at an experiential level, not merely cognitively, it brings about a great degree of fearlessness. Of course, to get to the root of the problem, we must first recognise the various factors that cause us to think in a particular way. We must attempt to understand our society and its culture better, and what it has evolved out of and into. For that sake I may go into history a touch in the coming chapters, nothing too drab, just the essentials.

Finally, I have written this book to provide solace and a way out for large numbers of sportspeople like me. We struggle to deal with the psychological hurricanes that accompany having to live day in and day out with feelings of lack. Even for a moment if you think all this is only for those who fail, please think again. Let me support this statement with the words of a New Zealand cricket legend: "I have shared the belief that I became riddled with cancer due to my toxic suppression of negative events throughout my life."[1]

This legend is Martin Crowe, who was amongst the most successful and celebrated batsmen of his time. Besides, he was also arguably one of the most inspirational captains New Zealand and probably the world has ever seen. All that considered, it was enormously brave of him to reveal the following truths about his life. In the article, he writes about two incidents that tormented him for decades.

The first one took place during 1992 World Cup semi-final, in which New Zealand played against Pakistan. One of Mr Crowe's 'demons,' which is part of folklore in his home country, was his decision to not take the field during Pakistan's innings. He was nursing a torn hamstring and had decided to rest, so he could recover in time for the final. NZ had set a stiff target and victory was clearly on the cards. But it was Mr Crowe's innovative captaincy that had led them to the semis and with him off the field, things didn't go well. NZ lost the crucial game. I remember watching that match as a kid and everyone including my dad said, "If Crowe had been on the field captaining, they would have won."

Crowe writes, "It was the one real chance for glory for my country, to lift the World Cup, and I was beside myself that I had misjudged the moment."[2]

The other incident is something I must present as captured by the author himself:

> February 4, 1991. Basin Reserve. I never forgave myself for getting out for 299 against Sri Lanka. Not a week would go by when I wouldn't be reminded of the one run I craved so much. It tore at me like a vulture pecking dead flesh. I did not know how to let it go, could never laugh at the absurdity of my anger. Ultimately it contributed to a dislike of myself, and to a notion that I was not worthy enough. I was desperate to be liked and I thought scoring big hundreds would suffice. I even thought one more run would be enough. I was staggeringly naïve to think so. I missed the entire point of life, how it should be appreciated.[3]

How can one suffer so much after making 299, you may question. Perhaps it happens more often than we think and no one can truly know what's going on inside another's head.

Mental suffering occurs for everybody, not just for those who don't make the grade. I have encountered many players with whom I would have most willingly traded places. Yet, they remain bitter about how things could have gone 'that much better' if a few things had turned out differently. Everyone, barring a rare few, has something or the other to crib about. When we're bitter, in other words when we resist the reality of the moment, we blind ourselves to new opportunities that may come up.

How passion becomes obsession one can never say, but both are degenerate forms of love that ultimately lead to dissatisfaction. Having said all this, I must clarify that this book is fundamentally a happy story. *It is as much about triumph as it is about defeat, but mostly it is about freedom from obsession.*

The sporadic displays of calmness in my career have produced extraordinary performances. If I could trade in my natural ability for calmness, I would do so because with calmness comes clarity, presence of mind and even-mindedness with which I could do anything. My mind was constantly journeying towards calmness, and calmness only came with performance. That was the irony and also the struggle. But it never came naturally; it took great effort and subconsciously I never trusted my mind to be calm. It had yet to be exposed to a teaching or an experience that altered it fundamentally

Since it's "All in the mind," let me start at the top and walk you through how it all unfolded.

But before I begin, a few notes:

- Most generalisations have been made by observing facts. It must be kept in mind that there are exceptions to most generalisations, however rare.
- When I use the word 'he,' no gender bias is advocated or implied.
- The book is divided into two parts. The first part (till chapter six) talks about common problems – the challenges, trials and frustrations I faced in trying to succeed in cricket with lofty ambitions. The second part presents solutions and details some triumphs.
- Wherever necessary, I have referred to scholarly work of authorities on various subjects to substantiate the points that I am making.

1. Formative years at Lovedale

MY CRICKETING journey began at a height of 7,000 feet in the Nilgiris, or 'The Blue Mountains,' as they are poetically known. The dream that I would one day represent my country took shape in Lovedale, a small town a few kilometres from the quaint and charming mountain-top town of Udagamandalam (Ooty) in Tamil Nadu. The British who developed the area called it 'The Queen of Hill Stations.' The founder of Ooty, John Sullivan, once wrote the following lines describing the splendour of the 'Neilgherry Hills':

> This is the finest country ever...it resembles I suppose Switzerland more than any other part of Europe...the hills beautifully wooded and fine strong springs with running water in every valley.[4]

I spent eight years of my early life atop these hills, three of them in Lena School (classes one to three) and five more (classes four to eight) in the glorious and incomparable setting of the Lawrence School, Lovedale.

The beauty of the place is indeed breathtaking – in retrospect. Sadly all this magnificence never registered, for I had little or no appreciation for sublimity. How could I? My brother and I were placed in boarding school at the tender age of five, ensuring that the picturesque Lovedale and Sigur Ghats leading up to the school meant only one thing – separation from our parents. The sorrow that accompanied the separation was simply too much for our fragile hearts to bear.

I was fortunate I had my brother for company, but it was still extremely hard. At that age your parents are your world, and what you want most is to be with them more than anything. Spending eight months a year away from them was traumatic, to say the least.

Of course, to save myself from attracting the ire of my folks, it's only fair that I mention why we were sent there. My father is an agriculturist (like most Kodavas) and worked for a large plantations company that posted him in rather remote locations around South India. His job involved routine transfers and there were no good schools around. Hence our parents had to put us in a boarding school. It was in our own interest they said, and it probably was.

However, back then I really thought it was an evil act. I vividly recall being dropped off at school for the first time. My mother handed me over to the teacher who showed me to my desk. I sat down knowing fully well that I wouldn't be seeing my Ma for the next four months.

I started howling away in my seat as my mother then proceeded to drop my brother off. When she was returning, I saw her through the gap in the classroom door and started running towards her crying and screaming, "Don't go, Ma." I saw that my mother was crying too and my father was firmly holding her hand, lest she run towards me.

Just as I was reaching the door, the class teacher got me and held me firmly as I watched my parents leave. I reacted so violently that I ended up hitting the poor teacher on her face. I can't remember who she was, but I sure hope she has forgiven me.

Homesickness is a terrible thing. Once it grips you, it never really leaves, especially at a young age. I experienced it right through my years at Lovedale. Needless to say the teachers in both these schools did their best to create a loving, homely environment, and that made things a lot easier.

THE CRICKET BUG BITES

I have a vivid recollection of first holding a cricket bat at age seven. It was the day before our holidays were to begin and the most anticipated time of the year. Most children had already gone home so Lena School wore a dull look, with just a few of us still left waiting for our parents.

To kill time we normally played football. But that day, one of the boys said he had seen a cricket bat in a dusty room in the main block. So off we went and found the bat. We took the bat and rushed back to the playground to play a new sport – cricket.

My earliest memory of playing cricket comes flying back to mind – my first lofted straight hit. The ball came off the middle of the bat, flew over the blue silhouette of the Nilgiri mountains and soared into the clear Ooty sky. The ball then hung in the air for a moment, before obeying the laws of gravity and dropping right back to the playground.

An orthodox coach would probably scoff at the shot, but I was thrilled. As most batsmen know, when the ball hits the middle of our bats, there is no feeling that comes close. And it's that feeling we become addicted to. I remember how satisfying it felt and from that day on, I was hooked to the game.

That shot earned me the admiration of the entire group. All I did in the holidays that followed was play cricket, most of the time with my brother (himself a good cricketer) and the children of our domestic help.

Early conditioning

Another incident cemented my association with cricket. It occurred one afternoon in a bungalow situated at the foothills of Sabarimala, a very popular pilgrimage centre in Kerala. Sabarimala is the abode of Lord Ayyappan whom my father named me after, as he is a staunch believer.

My dad is an ardent cricket buff and even now often speaks of his college cricketing days. That afternoon in the bungalow, he was in front of the television watching a match. As I was rushing out to play, he called me saying, "Come Baba (my pet name), look at this boy, Sachin Tendulkar. He's only 16 and is already playing for India."

My father seemed completely blown over by the kid and his achievement. At that moment I remember thinking, "I want my father to feel like that about me one day." Through repeated instances with both my immediate and extended family, I began to wrongly believe that there was nothing more to life than cricket. At family get-togethers, conversations livened up when the topic moved to the game and everyone seemed to be in awe of Indian cricketers. No other topic was as keenly discussed as sport.

Passions would often rise as my uncles, all alpha males, shared their sporting experiences and viewpoints with great gusto. Sporting stars were glorified and given a God-like status. The men of our family are primarily testosterone driven with very athletic bodies. Like my father, they too were very good sportsmen. One of mother's brothers almost played hockey for India, but an untimely knee injury had put him out of the reckoning.

All in all, it was a macho family environment, and sport is the ideal outlet for that machismo. Even outside of our family the milieu resonated with the same message. There was no escaping it. Sporting stars were idolised, and as such the proposition of becoming one was extremely attractive. But of course like in most Indian families, our mothers mostly wanted us to study and eat well.

Nonetheless, when I learnt I had the talent, there was only one way my life was headed. This was also true of my brother and two cousins who were similarly talented and influenced. We enjoyed natural athletic ability and the physical strength of our ancestors, warriors who had fiercely defended our lands. We are emotionally charged, very aggressive and possess lots of pride. Most times, response to pressure was in tune with this character.

In summary, I was born into a family, a society, a culture, and a country where conditions are such that I, like many other Indians, inherited a passion for cricket. By a process of social osmosis our minds naturally gravitated toward the sport. It's no wonder why young Indians until recently rarely played any other sport.

During our formative years, we breathe in our environment. A lot of what we take in is healthy and essential, but society also promotes limitations and at that age you cannot always discriminate: you just take in the whole lot. We unwittingly acquire a reflex way of thinking and feeling.

In fact neuroscientists such as Marco Iacoboni at the University of California (Los Angeles), have argued that mirror neuron systems or 'smart cells' in the human brain (in the pre-motor and inferior parietal cortex) are activated both when we perform a certain action and also when we observe someone performing that same action.

In other words it "collapses the distinction between seeing and doing." His book *Mirroring People: The Science of How We Connect to Others* claims mirror neurons play an important role in social cognition.[5]

Early leather-ball cricket

Lena School was a feeder to the grand Lawrence School, which was spread over 700 acres. So after completing my 3rd standard at Lena, I shifted over to Lawrence. My new school had three distinct blocks – Prep, Junior and Senior. The 4th, 5th and 6th standards were housed in Prep block, the 7th and 8th in the Junior block and the 9th, 10th, 11th and 12th standards in the Senior block.

I love the school's motto, 'Never Give In,' because it can be applied to any walk of life. Lawrence had a very vibrant sporting culture and placed strong emphasis on discipline. Our entire day was very regimented, almost military-like. We were woken up at 5.30am, given bun and tea, and made to go 'cross country' in the biting cold.

I enjoyed this aspect of the school and took part in all the sports (barring squash) on offer: cricket, football, badminton, hockey, athletics, basketball, tennis, table tennis, gymnastics, and swimming. And I played them all decently well, giving me excellent physical grounding.

One drawback was that I could not focus only on the sport of my choice. I had to follow the school's seasonal sporting calendar, and that meant playing all sports, not just cricket. Boys were divided into four houses named after the mountain ranges – Aravalli (my house), Vindhya, Sumeru and Nilgiri. Every few weeks, the houses would face-off against each other. Based on these performances, the school teams were drawn up.

In the five years that I was at Lawrence, I won the 'Best Athlete' for three consecutive years. But of all the sports, it was cricket that I enjoyed most. I just loved playing it with proper cricketing gear and a leather ball, like the big boys.

Mr Jaffer, our mathematics teacher, doubled up as the team coach for prep school. He was a very enthusiastic cricketer himself and made things interesting for us by constantly comparing us to international cricketers. He would encourage us giving compliments like, "You bowled that ball like Wasim Akram," or, "You played that shot like Sachin Tendulkar."

Those days, my heart would beat with great excitement and joy at the very prospect of playing the game. When the cricket season was on, I never felt homesick. It was a wonderful escape from all that. I was perpetually energetic and even when I was in class I would only think about playing.

Subconsciously, the game was becoming my only source of joy. Through school I hardly ever concentrated during class hours. But I always passed exams by going all out at the last minute and troubling my academically inclined friends to help me.

Every year, the school would invite coaches from the Bengaluru-based Brijesh Patel Cricket Academy (BPCA) to conduct a week-long coaching clinic – this was the 'funnest' time of the year. My dad had told us stories of how he had witnessed Mr Patel (who had represented India) tackling the spin of V V Kumar in the Buchi Babu tournament. Imagine how thrilled I was when I heard that Mr Patel himself was coming down to coach us! One evening, Mr Patel asked for a bat and knocked a few balls. Even after retirement he stroked the ball effortlessly.

Among other coaches, Mr Maney and Mr Kamal Tandon were my favourites and we received good coaching from them. Mr Maney also suggested that my brother and I go over to Bengaluru if we were serious about giving cricket a shot. He was extremely encouraging. I innocently asked him, "Sir, will I play for India?" He responded saying, "That I don't know. All I can say is you will become a very good cricketer."

My first match

In 6th standard, Mr Jaffer made me team captain for the inter-school competition that was approaching. He then asked us, "Who wants to open the batting?" I instantly raised my hand, along with a few others. He said, "Ok, you have to prove that you are worthy of that position. Play 24 balls without getting out." I did so and he said, "You will open tomorrow as you have proved yourself."

I was delighted because I was also bowling at the time, and this made me both an opening batsman and bowler. I would be in the game right from the start. Excited about the morrow, I could hardly sleep. The match was to take place at 'Middle Flats,' a ground that was located right below the Senior block. The match, 20 overs per side, was against a school called Breeks.

I lost the toss and Breeks decided to bat. I opened the bowling and picked up eight wickets – Breeks were bowled out for a paltry 32 runs. I then opened the batting, very confident after the bowling performance. I made 29 not out and we won the game within an hour and a half. I became a bit of a hero in school after this success. Teachers, students and staff congratulated me and put me on a pedestal. It was an immensely gratifying feeling.

The next match was the following day against a school named Laidlaw – our traditional rivals. In what was an away game, we won the toss and I scored 48 (a boundary counted for just two runs). We destroyed their much hyped leg spinner and posted a huge score, so much so that an official from their side came out with a tape and measured the length of the wicket. He then said the wicket was too long, and that's why their star spinner was not finding his length. It shows the craze that is cricket in India. We went on to win the tournament.

Those early years of cricket were so much fun. I played out of pure love, energy and feared nothing. The mind was innocent and had never known the 'fear of failure.' However, when I got out on 48, it was because my mind started thinking of how to raise the bat and celebrate the approaching half century. Till that moment I was just enjoying the batting, and the experience was pristine.

I recall Mr Jaffer telling one of the staff members, "This boy has courage, if you put him in front of Javagal Srinath also he will play." Another big compliment I received was courtesy our charismatic Principal Mr Dev Lahiri, who came to watch a match. While my teammates were getting out chasing a paltry total of around 90 runs, I offered resistance.

When I returned to the pavilion, Mr Lahiri said, "Looks like only one Lawrencian knows how to bat. Well batted son." Later that year I got the 'Best Batsman' award and he presented me with the trophy. I also remember our super seniors Nithin Abraham and Rohan Timblo, excellent cricketers themselves, saying some very flattering things.

The praise and attention that I earned after these performances made me feel on top of the world. I loved the attention. I was swept off my feet by these feelings and unconsciously began brainwashing myself into thinking that only performance in cricket could make me feel that way. My first brush with failure only heightened that feeling.

My first sporting failure

When I was in prep school, I played hockey as a forward and was very successful in our inter-house matches. Fast as I was on my feet, it really helped me get through defenders and score goals. But in junior school I wanted to try my hand at goal keeping. It was a time when I thought that I could never fail.

So in 8th standard I became a goalkeeper thinking it would be fun. I thought that if I stood at the post, nobody would be able to pass me and a loss was never on the cards. This was the confidence I had in myself. I was not in a big city, where you are easily humbled when you see talent at every corner. Before that game I was running around saying, "The world is my playground," as my father had recently bought a Mahindra Armada; if I remember correctly, that was the slogan they were using in the advertisements.

On that fateful day, I was all padded up with a stick in hand. Towards the dying minutes of a hard-fought game, the score line read 0-0. The rival house was advancing an attack, but at the top of the D, their forward was stopped well by our defender and the ball came rolling in my direction at snail's pace – as Geoffrey Boycott would have said, even my mother could have kicked that ball away.

Filled with hubris, I went to give the ball a good kick and dismiss it from my presence. What ended up happening was that I missed the ball completely, and their forward got around me and scored an easy goal. We were favourites to win and my mistake cost us the game.

The aftermath of this incident is something that shook me to my foundation and left me with deep mental scars. When I returned to the dorm, my teammates surrounded me on all sides as I sat on my bed, sullen. They proceeded to blame me for the loss, which they had already done on the ground. But in the dorm, things turned ugly. They cursed me, got personal, called me names, and said some downright spiteful things.

This was my front row ticket to humiliation, of how human beings are capable of such nasty behaviour. There was also a 'batch fight' concept where if someone was not liked, the whole class or batch would gang up and heap sorrow by castrating him socially.

This incident was an eye opener. I had always succeeded at sports and the moment I failed, I was pounced on and destroyed by the very people who were praising me. But barring a few genuinely devious minds, most of my classmates were perfectly good souls.

The contrast between success and failure is stark and extreme. There is an old saying that, 'Success has a thousand fathers but failure is an orphan.' I felt orphaned not only on that day, but on numerous occasions in the years that followed. Of course we were only a bunch of 13-year-olds and at that age, everything was like life and death.

After I completed 8th standard, my family moved to Madikeri in Kodagu, where I spent two years at a school called Kodagu Vidyalaya. Still, there was no cricket to play all year round.

Kodagu and Mangalore Zone

Here I was exposed to the Dronacharya of Kodagu – the venerated Mr Shankar Swamy who painstakingly coached me. He laid a sound technical foundation to my batting that no doubt came in handy when I played in Bengaluru. He also taught me yoga.

In my new school, I captained the team and won the inter school competition, making two consecutive unbeaten half-centuries (15-over contests). I remember walking back home thinking, "God I hope I could play more matches." The next match I played was after six months and I would often grieve about this. I also took to wicket-keeping during this time.

The monsoons are severe in Coorg and wipe clean more than four months of the calendar. Even during these rains my mother would throw over 100 balls at me, besides the practice my father gave me, in a small indoor patch. She did so for weeks before stopping, saying her arms were getting muscular. I tried convincing her that they were looking all right, but it didn't work.

I moved to Bengaluru the following year, and joined both BPCA and KIOC (Karnataka Institute Of Cricket) that is run by Mr Irfan Sait.[6] Most importantly, I finally got to enjoy year-round cricket.

In that time I also played for Mangalore Zone (Under-16) and the Karavalli Academy; for the first time I played matches in Bengaluru. The wide pool of talent intimidated me, but in my first match on turf I managed to score 56 against Dharwad. The match was played on the KSCA 'B' grounds, and it was a big thrill when Rahul Dravid walked by and I was able to get his autograph.

In the semi-final game, I had been told by our manager that the selectors were keeping an eye on me. In the finals, we were 44/5 chasing 270 odd runs against President's XI. I was put down five times en-route to an unbeaten 132, but it was still a century and I had batted bravely. Eventually, that knock earned me a place in the state Under-16 side. It was purely a combination of energy, enthusiasm, longing, innocence, hard work and grace that saw me break into the team.

I was honoured to be a state player and now had an image to live up to. Even though I never played a single game, I was proud and enjoyed touring as part of the Karnataka U-16 state team. I thought things would gradually progress and I would realise my dream, if I continued to work hard and did all the things required of me. Indeed, I worked extremely hard but things later turned out very differently.

I joined and played the 1st division league for three clubs at various times – Jawahars,[7] Swastik Union, and BUCC. I also captained my college team and in a match smashed 27 runs in one over. When I reached my century and raised my bat to an ovation, I felt an intense explosion of never before experienced happiness. It never left the whole day. To me the event simply reinforced the message that only cricket could bring about that level of joy.

A few years later, I represented the D Y Patil Group in Mumbai. Around the same time, I started a software company with a friend, to be able to continue playing post age 23 since I had yet to make it to the top. At age

26 I left the company, selling my stake for a reasonable sum. I finally lived my dream of focusing only on cricket without having to juggle it with other commitments.

The years seemed to fly by. I never took holidays. Like a madman, I played, practiced and prioritised cricket over everything else. I felt guilty if I did anything that is considered 'normal' for a growing adult. I believed that I had to sacrifice 'normal' to reach the top.

Overall, ages 16 to 26 were filled with disappointments, failures, frustrations and setbacks, interspersed with a few rare successes (when I was picked as a Ranji Trophy probable at age 19). Moreover, the only thing that mattered till I was 28 was success in cricket; nothing else existed or meant anything.

The early enjoyable days of cricket became a faint and weak memory. On one hand, I felt like I was running after a train that had left the platform, and on the other I strongly felt that things would miraculously turn in my favour. Peace came only when I freed myself from both these notions.

There was always something that seemed to pull me down. Yet I kept going. I wanted to take my journey to its logical conclusion. Each year I only worked harder. I wanted to return to enjoying the game and make my peace with it by fixing all the 'fault lines' in my thinking. While I take responsibility for succumbing to these pressures, I was only able to forgive myself after I had an epiphany of sorts when playing in Mumbai.

I understood there was no point holding myself accountable for every little thing. There are various factors that interact in making one's journey successful. Some of these we control while the others we can't. The inspiration to write this book has come from this understanding and with a hope that it may help those in similar situations.

Our attitudes, thinking, fears, pressures and resulting actions are not entirely our own. They emerge from certain conditions in society that mould our personality, motives and thinking. To know this is the first step, or entry-level knowledge towards understanding oneself. I want to share my findings on the various factors that whip the mind, heaping pressure on it, pressure it often buckles under.

I wondered for the longest time how my free spirited and innocent mind capable of so much, piled burden upon itself, killing its creativity and vitality in the process. How did I take something that was so dear to me and destroy it? How did I pervert the game I loved, by turning it into a medium to acquire renown, eminence and attention?

In answering these questions, I stumbled upon an intelligence that helped me overcome all these conditions and return to purely loving this game. An intelligence that is indigenous, that since antiquity has been considered a part of this nation's bloodstream. Yet it somehow lay hidden. *And how the game I loved most would be instrumental in revealing it.*

2. Exposure to city life

IN THE PREVIOUS CHAPTER, I described how the joy I felt while playing cricket as a youngster diminished with time. Perhaps circumstances off the field contributed in some way to the frustrations faced on it. Let me explain.

"The city kills your innocence," my cousin told me as I was leaving Kodagu for Bengaluru. I didn't think much of his counsel at the time; I was simply eager to get to Bengaluru. It's in the big cities alone where one learns the tricks of the trade. It's where most journeys towards realising God-given temporal talents culminate.

I reached Bengaluru in 1999 and my arrival coincided with the dot com revolution and the outsourcing boom that hit Bengaluru particularly hard, making it the IT (Information Technology) capital of the country. Naturally, a lot of us got swept up in the boom; many of my friends skipped college to do graveyard shifts and other part-time opportunities that had sprung up. It benefitted us in many ways – the money got us much-needed financial independence, confidence, purchasing power and freedom. It also drove the entrepreneurship and consumer spirit and attracted many industries to set up shop in the city.

The influx was so great that Bengaluru's infrastructure was caught unawares. In a couple of years, all the two-way traffic lanes surrounding my house became one-way. To this day, the city's infrastructure continues to be on a ventilator. No one asks the question, "How do the citizens cope?"

Everyone in my circle was getting richer, faster, and you could say happier as well. Our mindset and attitude became that of the marketplace, but that's why we got richer some may argue. At what cost was all this happening?

There were narratives and counter narratives about whether this was good for us or not. There were those who questioned reckless globalisation as threatening the basic moral, cultural and social underpinnings of our society. And there were those who argued that this money, if used well, could lift India out of poverty. The corporate world echoed the purple prose of how globalisation brings the world together as cultures intermingle, besides the obvious economic benefits. Both sides were right in some ways and both were also wrong in some.

Regardless of one's perspective, one thing is for sure. Corporate organisations work with a one-pointed agenda: they do first what is best for their bottom line – profit, money and wealth creation. And in doing so, moral, social and cultural nuances are cast aside. The boom was a result of American companies looking for cheaper labour in India that would significantly boost their profits; they shipped jobs here for that reason alone. It's no secret. Along with their jobs, their thinking and culture too became mainstream.

Soon after my final semester exams in college, I worked a short while in the front office of a multinational credit card servicing company. One evening, everyone on the floor celebrated a credit card loan that a salesperson sold at 33% interest. It was put up on the notice board as being worthy of emulation. Unwittingly the message that was being put out was, "Take notice of the new target you have to beat."

Now when you sell a loan at such high interest rates, two things obviously happen: 1) The company gets richer which is its main objective and 2) The person who sold the loan also gets richer because the company bosses consider him a champion salesman, and give him rewards and status.

They promote him or her to team leader; with this new position comes more wealth, respect, attention, power, importance and a sense of fulfilment. So subconsciously all ideas of contentment or happiness get tied to attaining wealth and reward. This sends a strong signal to the rest of the employees. As a policy this is not strictly immoral, because it can be argued that the company has its responsibilities to meet and without profit it can't meet any of them, including the salaries of its employees.

Sell, sell, sell becomes the only goal. If you can't convince, confuse! But make the sale. Everyone in the organisation is conditioned to do exactly that and the mind gets caught up in the bazaar. This culture seemed to remove compassion from the system and replace it with opposite values. Whatever remained was merely trained humility or mock modesty, unreal and synthetic in nature. No one took a moment to think of the plight of the person who that loan was sold to.

I must clarify that I am no communist. As I've said earlier, I have founded a business myself and am a beneficiary of the system. Besides, there is a lot one can learn from the West. Being developed nations, their professionalism and work ethic are worthy of emulation. Here I am simply bringing out certain facts to point out that the change was not happening in a balanced or moderate way. We increasingly found ourselves in a culture of excess, a culture that strongly fostered a 'never be satisfied' attitude that causes so much pressure and stress on both mind and body.

THE 'EQUATION'

Here's the 'Equation' that emerges from the trends of marketplace culture.

Wealth + Fame = Status + Success + Happiness.

I will henceforth refer to this connection as the 'Equation'. It acted as a springboard that brought forth certain mental qualities or thought processes that were responsible for a lot of the mental pressures I faced both on and off the field.

Historically, the strength of India has been its simplicity and idealism, and this 'Equation' was delivering a body blow to these pillars. The need of the hour was to balance the 'bread-winning' materialism of the West with the cultural richness of our ancestors.

The problems that can accompany a single-minded drive to wealth and power are well known. In a function hosted by the Tumkur University, where he was conferred honorary professorship, His Holiness the Dalai Lama said:

> The root of all evil is wealth. As wealth increases, greed increases, so does a sense of competition to earn more and more. This often gives rise to distrust and suspicion, which brings about fear and often creates frustration and anger that leads to violence.[8]

Regardless of our individual backgrounds, most of us meet this condition at some stage and our minds are influenced by it. As long as the motives remain pure there is no issue, but it's when lust replaces love that the troubles start.

The common narrative is that to 'come up' in life, one cannot afford compassion and that all wealthy people are corrupt. However, I believe people who work hard, dream big and take risks have a right to an opulent lifestyle; one must never grudge them that, for their ambitions and visions create opportunities that help millions.

Developing countries like India need capitalists, but most importantly we need them to be compassionate. We can survive only when the wealthy share their wealth with the less fortunate. I believe there is a term for it – compassionate capitalism (practiced by both Bill Gates and Warren Buffet). We need truly compassionate people to lead industries. I don't think compassion can ever be institutionalised, it must come from within.

How is all this relevant to sport, you may ask. The reality is that large corporates and politicians are involved in sport today, and their psychologies contribute to the conditioning of a sportsperson's mind. *Man is a social animal, and no mind, no matter how insulated, exists in a vacuum.* It is influenced by the values that drive society – by both their vigour and infirmities. With an open mind, when we analyse what these conditions are, we can better understand ourselves.

Coaches, parents, administrators and politicians (who run most of the sporting bodies in India) are often driven by the 'Equation.' Hence, they begin to look at players as profit-loss statements and not as human beings. This can cause a lot of psychological trauma for the players.

By getting to the root of the problem, I became aware of not only the values that were driving my thinking and behaviour, but also that of others. Constant work on myself helped me overcome some negative patterns, and brought me closer to enjoying the game with childlike enthusiasm once again.

I would like to go into this issue in some more detail and analyse the factors that play such an important role in shaping our minds and our destinies.

Values emerging from the 'Equation'

The mind today is surrounded with ideas that program it to acquire, aspire, and never be satisfied. For sportsmen, some of these values are foremost obstacles to optimal performance and the net effects are:

- *Result oriented mindset* – The end justifies the means. The process and the values that drive it are disregarded as irrelevant, as long as the end-result is obtained. Happiness is linked to reward.
- *Identity crisis* – We cannot distinguish between who we are and what we do. Our identification with this world is tightly bound to what we do to earn a living. Quite often, the reference point for validation is external, not internal. Therefore all mental energy is directed outwards.
- *Excessive individualism or personality built on wrong knowledge* – Overdue importance given to personality or one's image.

- *Greed, sophistication and impatience* – Simplicity and patience are no longer virtues that are celebrated or respected. Wealth and acclaim are admired instead.
- *Poor quality of education, teachers, role models and leadership* – Education and teaching are market-centric and not virtue-centric while leadership fails to inspire confidence. All knowledge is meant to further personality.
- *Lowest common denominator* – Intense feelings of competition and one-upmanship. Idealism receives a body blow.

When you apply this to cricket, wealth takes the form of runs, wickets and catches – statistics also known as performance. And the status of a player in sport is naturally linked to performance or the logo he wears on his shirt. *Sport then is also a pursuit of wealth in a different form and attracts all the conditions mentioned.*

As a result of all this, my mental and emotional programs were stuck in a pattern, leading to a crude one-dimensional system of thought.

The effect of the 'Equation' on personality or identity

Who am I, Ashwath Aiyappa?

When I look at this question, living in the midst of a society where affluence is at the heart of all pursuit, I get the following answer:

> I have represented my state in junior cricket. I have been told I am talented. I have earned some recognition and money playing the game and therefore will call myself a cricketer. By identification with this, I become somebody, someone of importance and relevance. And with an even stronger identification with the cricketer I aspire to become, the idea grows in strength. I dedicate my entire life to sustaining and furthering it, because without it, I am nobody.

From this my personality or image was born, and this is how I thought of myself. I discovered later that this narrow identification caused all the mental gymnastics that would eventually culminate in pain and sorrow. Perhaps all psychological suffering that humanity faces is a consequence of human mind/behaviour being largely established in personality.

The word 'personality' itself is derived from the Greek word 'persona,' which means mask. A mask is something with which you play a role and discard – technically it is a dead thing. We completely identify with our masks and constantly feel the need to empower it. It could well be that there is something that lies beyond the mask.

Values that drive personality

In Ooty, I played the game out of joy and free of agenda. Playing with that spirit I ended up playing for Under-16 Karnataka in my very first year. But as years passed, I started to visualise the glitz and glamour of the sport, the money, the endorsements, the fame, the attention from the opposite sex and so on. Most of my energies were frittered away on these sorts of things and less and less on the game itself. I still loved the game, I knew that deep down, but it got so covered up. Gradually I had turned the game into a vehicle to deliver opulence, but I wasn't the only one.

I recall a recent incident in which a nutritionist was invited by our coach to speak to us. At the time, this nutritionist was also advising a prominent national cricketer. After giving us some valuable insights on eating habits he added, "Do you know which car [the famous cricketer] drives?" When we said we didn't know, the nutritionist said, "He drives a Mercedes Benz so if you want to drive a Mercedes please make sure you start by eating right."

Whatever the profession, people seem to be similarly motivated, be it business, politics, or cricket. Visible symbols of success are worshipped and this has far-reaching consequences. Society's mind is such that it legitimizes only happiness born out of achievement associated with tangible material benefits. This is called 'success.' Without these prerequisites, you don't qualify to be happy or deserve to be called successful. All these ideas are below the surface of our minds, in our subconscious, and subtly operate and interfere from there.

Idealism has fallen while corruption has grown to never before seen levels. I recently attended a hockey match at the end of which a local, corrupt, and wealthy politician handed out the prizes. Everyone in the audience clapped. By the very act of clapping we declared that we condoned all his misdemeanours, and applauded his position of power and influence.

Though the 'Equation' is a major and common conditioning factor, it is not the only one. At different ages we are subject to different pressures. Broadly these are:

- Age 15 – Exam pressure or urge to be free from parental control.
- Age 18 – Girlfriends or boyfriends and peer pressure.
- Age 22 – You are looked at as a cow that must start producing milk.
- Ages 25-30 – Wealth, status, position, power struggles and marriage pressures intensify.
- Age 35 – Consolidation of the above in addition to working and dealing with family pressures; health issues may show up.
- Age 40 – all this leads to a mid-life crisis and the circus goes on.

At every stage there is pressure, as effort is generally driven by lust or craving. And the offspring of any pursuit so driven is *fear*, which could typically fall under one of these two categories:

- *Fear* of losing what one has
- *Fear* of not getting what one wants

When I am relevant, I fear becoming irrelevant and so I will do whatever it takes to stay relevant. When I am physically fit or in good form, I fear getting injured. When I am in the team, I fear being replaced by competition. When I receive attention and fame, I fear jealousy. When I am wealthy, I fear penury. When I have knowledge, I fear someone will know more and break my arguments. In beauty there is the fear of becoming ugly, in love is the fear of being cheated upon.

When subject to the 'Equation,' everything becomes filled with fear and insecurity. This mental framework acts as a safe-house in which fear lurks, preparing the ground for attack. It creeps upon us in pressure situations and we often succumb. The same fear shred me to pieces on several occasions. The really good players know how to deal with these pressures, but it is a rare mind that goes beyond it all.

Changing times, changed values and lifestyle

In those ten years, between 2000 and 2010, a new non-formal social and moral order termed as 'progressive' emerged, and challenged many old conventional ideas and beliefs. The old ones were the many time-tested values of our parents that came to us mostly from religion, culture and tradition. The new ones were perhaps coming out of our television sets from the glamour driven masters of the material world. Each had two distinctly different ideas of society, one based mainly on our families/roots and the other based on principles of success and wealth.

Both had their pluses but as always, finding the middle path in changing times was a challenge. Even our elders fell prey and pushed their young ones too hard, advancing outcome-oriented thought processes. To get away from it all, a lot of us rebelled, indulging in mind-numbing, pleasure-seeking vices to distract ourselves.

The materialistic culture that breeds cutthroat competition penetrated all spheres of society. It made the Equation more explicit, causing a mass migration in support of the ideas that were coming from the West.

American sitcoms had a tidal wave influence on urban India. They set the tone and influenced all, from the way we spoke and interacted with one another to the media and the way scripts were written for movies and advertisements. Almost everything was laced with lazy titillation meant to seduce the now richer middle class out of their homes and into shopping malls. The net effect of the new order is that it kept our energies trapped in seeking pleasure alone.

Social networking sites made our lives a constant round the clock advertisement. Technologically we became advanced but what of our minds? We even called ourselves the 'fatafat' or 'instant generation.' The system was so designed that restraint and responsibility were outdated, and frivolity and greed was 'in.' The sensually charged environment was built to cultivate desire. And when there is craving, *no matter how trivial, the mind is always in a state of agitation.*

The 'never be satisfied with anything' attitude was fully exploited by advertisers. The definitions of need and want were continuously redefined for the consumer. A creative director of an online media agency told me, "We can always create a need when there is none." Without an alternative intelligence, the mind submitted to this conditioning and paid the price, getting tossed like a basketball between the extremes of pleasure and sorrow.

In my immediate circles, I saw our viewpoints on various issues gradually diverge and not always in a good way. We surrendered our idealism. I know that a bunch of us in college swore not to lose ourselves to the temptations of drugs, sex and alcohol. But we wound up not only doing these things but also doing so excessively. Tragically, I lost two of my very dear friends – one to substance abuse and the other to drunken driving.

The irony is the West is looking towards Asia for inspiration and ideas to revive or prevent collapse of their family structures, while we are aping them. Talking about the plight of the elderly in the UK, the country's health minister, Jeremy Hunt, recently said that his country needed to learn from Asian nations. He stated, "We find fairly horrifying, the number of elderly people who feel the TV is their best friend."[9] The young do not want to care for the old, it is seen as the government's responsibility. He added, "I am struck by the reverence and respect for older people in Asian cultures."

Although I might have sounded pessimistic, we do have with us the comforting words of the incomparable Swami Vivekananda:

> Shall India die? Then from the world all spirituality will become extinct, all moral perfection will be extinct, all sweet souled sympathy for religion will be extinct, all ideality will be extinct; and in its place the duality of lust and luxury as the male and female deities, with money as its priest, fraud, force and competition its ceremonies and the human soul its sacrifice. Such a thing can never be.[10]

The general decadence in the value system has happened because simplicity is no longer celebrated. It is easier to lead a happy life when you have fewer lifestyle demands. But the character of society that links wealth to status does not make this mode of living attractive.

Likewise in sport, the hardest thing to do today is to 'Keep things simple.' This is near impossible to do when there is so much riding on performance. Fear is bound to exist. It is harder for today's generation to keep things simple than it ever was.

OTHER FACTORS THAT PREY ON PERSONALITY

We have seen that the major emergent quality of society's conditioning is fear. However, other important forces do exist that influence our minds. One such is religion. Regardless of the religion dominating the psychology of a people – be it Hinduism, Islam, Christianity, Buddhism, Sikhism, Jainism, Zoroastrianism or Judaism – all espouse certain precepts.

Involving religion here is important, because from time immemorial it has conditioned human behaviour. When desperate, we all pray to our Gods to bail us out. All faiths have an idea of God and of what constitutes good and bad or right and wrong.

The very meaning of the word 'religion' is to bind or unite – this is the singular higher purpose it is meant to serve. Perhaps religion is meant to uncover the mask (personality) so you can realise your true potential, but certainly not to empower it.

Unfortunately, custodians of various religions have diluted that spiritual core and millions have fallen prey to its outer trappings. Today the immediately perceptible themes that *reflect our mental nature* are broadly the following:

- Division and difference
- Fear used to drive worship

Division and difference

I will share the rather shocking way in which the pervasiveness of this dawned on me. After an average season in Karnataka in 2010 I went to Tripura for a short while, playing for a club there and trying to make it to the Ranji level via that route. I met a cricketer who had come to play for the same club. He was a very devout practitioner of his religion (I don't want to name it). Knowing little of the faith he belonged to and being ashamed of the fact, I one day asked him to enlighten me.

In response to my request (he spoke in Hindi but I have translated it here in English), he said, "Fine, but I will tell you frankly." I replied, "That's what I want."

He said, "It is written in our book that if you do not belong to my faith there is no hope for you," and added, "The day you accept our faith all your sins are forgiven."

On hearing this, my first thought was "Can this be true?", and immediately thereafter I was angered by his insinuation. I saw it as a rejection of my faith and it clearly created a psychological divide between us.

I failed to understand how he reconciled that notion with the fact that almost 90% of his teammates belonged to another faith. And for team spirit, unity is essential. I could not balance that view with the wonderful experiences I had with some of my closest friends who were born into his faith.

All my education happened in institutions where right from pre-school to university, I was lucky to not find any trace of sectarianism. In fact it was quite the opposite. I remember the popular and habitually reinforced pronouncement of our guardian at Lena School. She would tell us, "All Indians are brothers and sisters, there is no difference between us."

Division should not be confused with diversity; diversity is essentially the same thing manifested in different form factors. That said, conflicts exist not just between religions but also within them in the form of class, caste, culture and region-based differences. And in each case, the divisions are because of differing ideas of God, ways of life or forms of worship that make people hostile towards another. Instead of practicing their religion's real precepts, people use the differences to create a divide and then define themselves on the basis of that difference. They all say, "We are better than them, so please join us."

In sport, we are taught about the '3 Ds' – Determination, Dedication and Discipline. But the message that society gives us is a different version of the '3 Ds' – Divide, Differentiate and Define.

There is a constant battle for supremacy – "I have decided my way is the only way and therefore I am superior," and alternative forms of thought are frowned upon. The '3 Ds' that drive our thinking and personalities come to us from multiple sources and not just religion. It could also be the competitive work-culture where performance is meant to create a differential, or from family background or the status one is born into. There could be several other reasons as well.

When you look around today, you see so much importance being given to personality, to individuals and not the whole system. The individual has emerged as supreme, above even family, team and country. Education too strengthens this idea. We are partially influenced by the Superman and Batman culture in which an individual alone fights all evil to restore good.

While we have a responsibility towards improving or bettering our talents, the process will be made simpler and more enjoyable if we can do so by recognising that we are all fundamentally products of the same clay. Failure to understand this truth causes all the ill feelings and bitterness towards others.

Fear used to drive worship

Besides my father, my maternal grandmother is a very devout Hindu. Her prayers, many of my uncles say, is what has kept the family safe and prosperous. Growing up, obeisance to the Almighty was compulsory for all her eight grandchildren. She made it a point to gather our restless bodies and tumultuous minds in the prayer room in an attempt to restore us to our proper rhythms.

She would make us face the hundred colourful manifestations of the Supreme before us, with strict non-negotiable instructions. She would then proceed to call out the name of each God, which we had to repeat after her. At times to instil faith, she would often tell us dreadful stories of the consequences of not being devout, a habit she continues even to this day.

I wish faith had come to me the way it does for her. It would have saved me a lot of mental suffering and God knows I needed it those years. Faith is a rare gift and a death knell to both doubt and even rationality. An over-enthusiastic rational mind poses question after question and doubt after doubt that can sometimes cripple performance.

The notion of an all-powerful God above, who can make all our dreams and wishes come true, gives us much solace. The exegetists tell us that if we petition Him with our desires by means of offerings or sacrifice, He will grant us all our wishes. The middlemen who treat religion as their exclusive domain often use fear as a tool to extract worship. And 'just in case they turn out to be right' we pray, so as to not attract God's wrath.

We again fear that if we don't worship Him, He may not give us what we want and instead heap suffering and misfortune. Ritual and customs are blindly followed, turning human beings into superstitious bigots. Thus, *fear becomes institutionalised.* The very custodians of various religions indulge in such false propaganda so they stay relevant.

It begs the question, can God really be of this nature? Let's imagine there is a God in the popular understanding of the term. You think He would want us to fear Him or love Him? You think he would want us to embrace values that cage the mind or liberate it?

I had an attitude problem when it came to God. I judged His worth on the basis of the rewards He gave me. When I did well, I would say, obviously it's my hard work that is responsible. But when I failed I would blame Him. After repeated desperate failed appeals and futile attempts to cut a deal to advance my cricket career, I decided that God does not exist. I did not say even a line of prayer for five years.

The rare exceptions who really love God, belong to a different category altogether. But mostly, reverence is out of fear, desperation or agenda and rarely out of love. This becomes another factor by which fear could potentially become a part of our psyche. When the very foundations of our personality are built on fear, it's impossible to be fearless. For how can one use fear to become fearless, just the way you can't clean dirt with dirt.

Now let's move on to another conditioning aspect of sport.

The politics and economy of sport

Why bring politics and economics into sport, you may ask. Well, I hate to break it to you, but nothing in this world is divorced from both these, and this necessitates establishing a connect. There are studies that link the political and economic situations of a country to medal tallies in the Olympics.

Very simply put, a country needs to have lots of money and a willingness to spend it on world-class coaches, support staff, infrastructure and facilities. Systems need to put in place to unearth, identify and develop talent as well as see it through to its potential. For this, we need a management team with vision, drive and noble intent.

The captivating nature of sport attracts all. The heads of most sporting associations are politicians. This institutes a certain culture and mind that reflects in all decision making. The Common Wealth Games (CWG) scam is only too well documented, where even toilet-paper was not spared.

After decades of such shenanigans, the IOC (International Olympic Committee) banned the IOA (Indian Olympic Association) – a huge national shame but a necessary one. We can only hope it returns cleaner. As I write this, the IPL is in all sorts of trouble, with a slew of scandals and corruption charges emerging.

The inimitable writer Mr Arun Shourie[11] says that political party bosses, while scouting for suitable candidates, look for the following qualities:

1. He must be an inconsequential person or 'knowledge proof' – a person with no special expertise or independent view so he remains entirely under the patronage of the party hierarchy. Party bosses fear the mix of intelligence and character, as it has the potential to wreak havoc. All they want is for the status quo to be maintained.
2. He must be a salivating person – lusting for the next position, so he will toe the party line.
3. He must be a compromised person (his family must be involved in some scandal or the other), so he is always vulnerable and party bosses can use this to hold him down.[12]

Doesn't this sound familiar? When such is the psychology of individuals at the helm, before long everybody is gripped by corruption. As bosses, they call the shots; their values and agenda become that of the organisation. And this finds a way into the intellectual and moral scheme of subordinates who are encouraged to align their thinking with that of their leader.

All that said, we do have upright politicians and leaders. It is perhaps because of their uprightness that the country continues to survive and have hope. We have seen how conditioning occurs and it applies to all institutions, where the trickledown effect is ever at play. Hence leadership is very important.

The characteristics of society are such that the personalities of citizens are often conditioned by values that are meant to deliver power and wealth. *This psychology is our driving force with which we set and chase goals. Education too largely provides the tools and intelligence to justify such an approach.*

Team sports unite

Having said all this, in the short time I was in Tripura, I noticed that the cricketer I spoke of earlier was a complete team man. Despite his views, he encouraged us all. He was there to further his career in cricket and so was I, and as a result we had to work together. Whatever our motives, the process of playing a team sport united us.

The flip side of ambition must also be appreciated. Like with sports, there are several new professions that have arisen on the back of strong economic development that offer similar opportunities to reconcile differences.

In pressure situations, players rally around one another not caring the least of a person's religion or skin colour in the quest for victory, and in doing so all apparent differences disappear. For example, football, basketball, rugby and other sports have acted as catalysts in bringing together people of diverse backgrounds in America and South Africa.[13]

When India won the cricket world cup in 2011, it felt like the whole nation won and not just the 11 who played. Many of us were on the road and people stopped cars and shook hands to say, "We did it." Amidst all the pluralism we became one. That's the power of sport.

Conclusion

There are several channels that condition our minds, but the end result of conditioning is limitation. A chained dog does not care if the chain is made of gold, because all he wants is to break free.

In the next chapter I talk about my experiences of playing league cricket in Karnataka.

3. Playing league cricket

GETTING SELECTED for the Ranji Trophy (state) side is not easy. There is an elaborate process by which players are picked. First, a player needs to perform well in the Sir Mirza Ismail[14] shield. This is a first division tournament in which 12 teams participate. The best players in this tournament and age group cricket are then picked to form four teams for an annual tournament called the Safi Darashah.

Based on performances in Safi Darashah, three teams are further picked for an All India tournament in Bengaluru hosted by the KSCA. Good performances in this tournament could result in selection for the Buchi Babu or Moin-ud-dawla[15] tournaments. Based on all these performances, the state side is named, and a similar process is followed by almost every state in the country.

Consistent performances in the Ranji Trophy catch the eye of Indian selectors. But if you're in Karnataka, playing for the state team itself is a mighty arduous task because Karnataka is a large state. And unlike other states, most notably Maharashtra[16] and Gujarat,[17] we have only one cricket team.

Needless to say, competition is fierce. Cricketers of the highest calibre and with no real failures sometimes have to sit on the bench. Each one of them could easily find a place in any other Ranji team in the country. It's about time the BCCI (Board of Control for Cricket in India) considers at least two teams for Karnataka and other large states.

Having shared the selection process, I'll now write about my own experiences.

The goof ups and missed opportunities

So far, I've played 12 continuous seasons of first division cricket for three different clubs.[18] I have witnessed several talented players who have suffered the same fate that I did, of not being able to make it to the top levels. The reasons are clear now. While revisiting those years is both painful and embarrassing, it must be done.

Let me start by describing events that unfolded in the only Safi Darashah game I ever played, so you get an even better understanding of how the brain capsizes under pressure. Prior to this match, I had warmed the benches for five games over two seasons before getting my chance.

The selectors were watching from a distance and I was eager to perform. I walked in to bat after we were reduced to 40 odd for four. I could hear the sound of my heart pounding in my chest, a feeling I've had many times in my career. My hands and legs were trembling, my mouth was completely parched and inside the helmet it felt a hundred degrees. I was not sure of myself, but strangely, the bat felt good in my hands. The bowler was hitting good areas, and this only increased the tension.

In that state of nervous excitement, I hit three beautiful boundaries and raced to 12 runs off 15 balls. I threw a quick glance to check to see if the selectors had taken notice. Just as I was feeling somewhat vindicated, I proceeded to do the dumbest thing. I jumped out of the crease the very next ball and wildly swung my bat at it. I missed the ball by some distance and looked back to see the keeper taking off the bails with ease.

Once again the monkey inside me emerged and enforced itself at an all-important time. It's funny how pressure tends to bring out one's true level of maturity. I knew I had only that one chance, and I was eager to score a million runs in that one innings. But the opportunity was not met with the temperament needed for the occasion.

Obviously, my preparation had been inadequate. I had always struggled with being impulsive and feared that side of myself, but I had put it away successfully for a couple of seasons. However, I found that it was still very much there, lurking below the surface of my conscious mind. *All the skill in the world is useless if you do not have a mind that allows you to express it.*

I walked back disgusted and my coach gave me a mouthful saying, "Why can't you just put your head down, score and go to the next level man." He too had watched me over the years and was keen to see me perform. I was shattered; I had lost a golden opportunity. A selector told me at lunch, "How can you play a shot like that and throw away all the hard work?" I was at a loss for words as I really could not understand it myself. As a friend of mine would jokingly say, "It was self-suicide."

Out of here, out of fear

The feeling of getting dismissed early in one's innings can be a horrible experience, especially when you are desperate to make runs. When a bowler beats your defences, you hear the sound of leather shattering wood. You turn around to see the stumps you were meant to protect lying dismembered. Your mind begins to fall apart.

To add insult to injury, you often hear the noise of 11 screaming and sometimes mocking players celebrate your downfall. You leave the field with the message, "You're not good enough, please leave the pitch right now." Often it's a dead, numb man who walks back to the pavilion. The most damage is done when you get out early in a game and have to sit and brood the entire day, with not much to do. That's when negativity feasts on your mind.

After a low score you really don't want anybody asking you, "How much did you score today?", but that's wishful thinking. I cannot tell you the number of times I have rung the doorbell and my mother has opened the door excitedly asking, "What happened, Baba?" With a heavy heart and never wanting to be the one to deliver bad news, I would inform her that I got out early. She would often get upset and say, "Why do you continue playing this game, it has given you so much pain, just leave it and do something else."

I would always put up a strong front and respond saying, "No Ma, I am ok. It's all part of the game." That was the standard line. In junior cricket, I would sometimes lie – I would add 10 or 15 runs to look better and hope my parents never found out.

The suffering was too much. But the real factors causing the agony were never addressed. Instead of facing the hurt head on, I covered it up with pleasure. Most players, including myself, indulged in frivolities to cover the pain. We would feign bravado, point fingers, talk down other players, and discuss women or Bollywood. Some simply used cigarettes or alcohol.

It took me a massive effort to get back on my feet and train continuously. Handling failure can be quite a task; there are days you wish you never woke up. To make matters worse, your teammates and coaches are not always empathetic; instead, you become the object of scorn.

The Australian journalist Greg Baum throws light on some of the factors that lead to depression. Below are excerpts from an article he wrote, following Jonathan Trott's exit from the 2013 Ashes in Australia:

> The explanation that resonates with me is Frith's description of cricket as a one-chance game. "Golfers, footballers, tennis players

and boxers all have an assurance that they have a chance to recover from an early defeat in the game, but cricket embodies uncertainty on the grand scale, and on a relentless daily basis."

A dismissed batsman, no matter how unlucky, vanishes from the game, sometimes for days. Brearley called it 'symbolic death.' Think of Trott in Brisbane: twice out early, in ways that were embarrassing for a Test batsman, leaving him for the rest of the match either to sit in the pavilion or trudge around the outfield, brooding over those humiliations.

It is one thing to know that you are only as good as your last game, another that that game never comes to an end. Except for two hours every week, a footballer always can train his mind on the next game. A cricketer cannot. Multiplied over matches and years, it is bound to have a deleterious effect.[19]

Many English cricketers including Trescothick, Yardley, and Harmison have suffered depression related illnesses. David Frith, author of two books on cricketers committing suicide, wrote:

> It seems to me that the long days of dedication which cricket demands by its often punishing format can wear a man down, especially when he doesn't know where his next run or wicket is coming from. A vicious circle is created: sleepless nights, worrying about the next match, brooding over recent failures, which can even seem like humiliations; followed by further nervous performance and an extension of the bad run of form or, perhaps worse still, bad luck, such as a bad umpiring decision against you. It is all very wearing.
>
> My book revealed some surprising statistics (all offered tentatively, for there can be no precise figures in this study): almost all the cricket suicides noted in my 2001 book were white Anglo-Saxons. Continuing research, however, has seen a new factor: there have been a number of attempted or completed suicides on the Indian subcontinent. The cause often seems to be inconsolable — perhaps slightly irrational — disappointment among youngsters after fail-

ure to reach the top of cricket's now-lucrative career ladder, with all the glamour and money on offer. [20]

As a youngster who often got out early, a flood of questions engulfed my mind: "What's going on?", "How do I break free", or fatalistically, "Here we go again."

For various reasons, my mind had yet to arrive at a value system or method that it could trust beyond doubt to deliver. It was easily influenced by opinion and suffered immensely from faulty perceptions. It reacted personally to on-field taunts and got into a habit of chasing windmills that often propelled worst-case scenarios into occurring. The more I defended myself against these mental states, the more they attacked and the more I came under their spell.

Even if I did well, it would be an intense struggle to discipline myself and combat the negative programs that had taken root in my mind. It was mentally and physically very draining, while for other players it seemed simple. I never lacked the skills; the difference was in attitude, thinking and preparation. There were thought processes or superstitions I seemed powerless against.

All this made the game I loved so much seem like an arduous task. The goal I had set myself was very high and I was nowhere near achieving it. I was living with feelings of lack, day in and day out. This attracted all kinds of burdensome thoughts and with no technique to combat them. I shamelessly gave into them all.

Sportspeople will tell you that our best game flows when our minds are kept simple, with as few thoughts as possible. In this state, the performance just happens, there is no making it happen; we are just a witness to the performance as it unfolds through us.

Decoding the monkey mind

In my early 20s I was super fit, the reason being that I trained well with an expert yoga and martial arts teacher, Mr Vijay Dhruve. However with regard to my mind, just about everything was wrong. The bane of my cricketing career, particularly my batting, was that I got out too often in the 20s and 30s.

The first 15 runs are the hardest for any batsmen but I made those very easily. A friend once joked with me, "You start off well and end up struggling." At the start my concentration would be sharp and I would be bubbling at the crease playing just one ball at a time. To overcome my self-imposed imaginary fears of another bowler's prowess and my imagined inability to deal with him, I would try and forcefully hit a few early boundaries. But after a while my mind would wander.

I did not know how to stay present or stick to the task of watching the ball for long periods. I always depended on runs for gratification and because of this I repeatedly faltered in my shot selection – an extremely important facet of batting.

If I made only 30 runs playing beautiful shots, I would often become insecure that I may not score 20 runs more. I was told I did not qualify to be happy with my strokes if it did not lead to a milestone. Invariably my father, managers and coaches would say, "What is the use of 30, you need hundreds to make it."

I would imagine all the players judging me and laughing at my inability to make big runs. And the following thought would often enter: "If I score 50 or 100, my folks will be proud; my club secretary and teammates will appreciate me."

This is true, but you cannot consistently make hundreds if you don't enjoy everything about the game, including the days you make 0 or 30. Sir Don Bradman, for all the centuries he scored, fondly recalled a 36 he once made.

Generally I found it hard to control the mind; if one ball bounced awkwardly, I assumed the next ball will also do the same, and would fail to play it on its merit. Many times I played the bowler and his reputation and not the ball he bowled. The focus was more on the opponents and less on my strengths.

I worked up bowlers in my own mind, gave them undue importance and they often got me out to very ordinary balls. Against easy bowling attacks, instead of cashing in, I would think, "Anyway nobody will count a score against a weak bowling attack. A good performance against them is hardly going to bring me any prominence." Thinking so, I would become uninterested. My mind lacked objectivity and discriminatory powers.

While wicket-keeping I would think, "If I make a mistake here or drop a catch, everyone will shout at me and blame me for the loss." Under pressure I sometimes completely shut down and lost presence of mind. When senior players shouted at me, instead of becoming more alert, I would become more nervous.

Also, if a competitor of mine did well, it somehow made it harder for me to play freely. I would feel deflated though I was not the only one whose feelings depended on the performance of others. One incident I remember is when a player called up the scorer in another match to find out if his rival had done well. When he learned that he had failed, he celebrated. Later that day he himself failed to make runs. I found this attitude among players who had gone on to play both Ranji Trophy and IPL.

Unlike my early cricketing days when I used to enjoy my cricket, around this time the nights before a game became unbearable. Everyone suggested visualisation and the technique was yielding positive results for a lot of them. I was never able to successfully visualise because only negative scenarios would form, no matter how hard I tried. I always imagined the bowler getting the better of me.

I imagined the feeling of guilt I experienced when going for practice after a low score. I feared that the opposition bowlers would sledge me and I would become tensed thinking I was incapable of handling it. I told myself if I couldn't feel truly confident, "I will fake it till I make it." In addition to trying to fake it, I became increasingly superstitious.

THE PLAGUE OF SUPERSTITION

Superstitious rituals would start building up from the time I began packing my kit for a game. I would think twice about which pair of whites to pack. I would look at a pair of trousers and before packing them, almost automatically the question would arise, "How much did I score the last time I wore these?" If it was a duck, I invariably never packed them. I was failing so much that almost my entire wardrobe reminded me of failure. All this sounds so silly now, that's because superstitions are really silly by nature.

Perhaps I was asking the wrong questions and looking at things the wrong way, for nobody ever held me guilty of not working hard. I also made an effort to show everyone that I was working hard to stay fit and all that. Perhaps perfect practice was missing.

I remember a close cricketing friend telling me, "You're super fit, but you need to do more skill work da." But the coaches told me that my skills were fine and all I needed to do was relax. So I chose to overrule what my friend had to say. Looking back, I can see that I was very caught up with what others had to say.

All the mental and emotional programs that I was subject to meant that I was unable to either keep things simple, stay in the present or enjoy myself. A former India batsman told a friend of mine, "Every time a batsman gets out, he tends to search for the fault in his technique or some other reason, but most often, the only reason he gets out is because he isn't watching the ball as closely as he should be." Cricket, like any other sport, can be made phenomenally simple.

I needed a method. I needed technical and tactical inputs. For some reason, I thought I must come up with these myself. The club that I represented unfortunately could not give me the insight I was craving. It was a loving club with some wonderfully well-intentioned people running it. They saw talent in me and gave me multiple opportunities to succeed. However, I failed more than I succeeded. Towards the end, every time I went into bat I began to feel as though I owed the club a million runs. That again only caused more pressure.

My club had yet to put a scientific coaching methodology in place. They were adamantly traditional in their approach and could not match the pace at which the game was changing. They said I was one of those players who worked too hard but could not translate that into performance. They said I thought too much about the game and that put excessive load on my mind. They said I had the talent but not the mind and that I was too impatient.

Over time, I subconsciously began to believe all this was true. It took a lot of work to break out of that. But I know now that it was not having a method that made me insecure, and this insecurity made me stress out.

Though no one stopped me, I felt that it was unethical to ask for help from anyone outside my club. My ego also played a role in stopping me. It would say, "I will make it on my own, I don't need anybody's help." Of course, this is not possible. When I met Dr Kinjal Suratwala[21] for the first time, I did not want to meet him in the KSCA clubhouse where everyone could see us. Basically I did not want people to know that I was taking his help.

The role of peer pressure

There is a saying, "Show me your friends and I will tell you who you are."

When you hang out with angels you become angelic, and you turn demonic when you consort with demons. Angels are selfless while demons are the opposite. The group of friends a person chooses to have is hugely important.

Off the field, we have some control over whom we want to surround ourselves with. But within the cricketing ecosystem we don't have that luxury. Handling friends and colleagues who are on a different wavelength can become very tricky. Mr Raghuram Bhatt[22] would often advise us, "After your practice just pick up your bags and go home." Invariably it is after the nets that players indulge in gossip and other distractions.

Unfortunately it is not just on-field action that can be traumatic. Cricketers, particularly junior cricketers, are vulnerable to downright appalling behaviour from their seniors. I want to share an incident that took place when I toured Chennai as a junior cricketer.

The tour was badly organised. Around 30 boys were herded into a dormitory like cattle and made to sleep on the floor. A few senior players – the bosses of the team – thought it would be 'fun' to collect everyone's sperm and pour it on those who were fast asleep.

Along with a friend, I refused to participate in this sordid 'game' and we were resented for not 'playing' along. Fortunately we both protected each other and this made things easier. My friend and I took turns to stay awake through the night and watch over the others to ensure nothing untoward happened. Needless to say, the lack of sleep affected how we played. Even a manager who was sent along with us was highly irresponsible. He would start drinking alcohol first thing in the morning.

This is an extreme example, I agree. But extremely bad behaviour needs to be eradicated. As a junior cricketer, I never wanted to complain about the terrible behaviour of seniors for fear of being ostracised. I never registered a formal protest because in addition to the fear of being left out, complaining is simply not something 'alpha males' do.

So I tried to blend in, in whatever way I could. On several occasions I did silly things simply to please others or to make them laugh and say, "Ashwath is really funny" or "Ashwath has a lot of guts."

The problem is that once you get slotted as a certain type of person, people refuse to change the image they have of you. They associate you only with that image. Even years later, when I meet some of them and don't behave in the manner they expect, they keep asking me, "What's up with you? All ok?" And I find myself having to cater to the image they have of me.

Therefore, it's better to be who you are. Don't pretend to be something you're not. All I am saying is, there is no need to do harmful things because of a fear of unpopularity. Banding together with like-minded people is a lot better and easier on the mind.

A word of caution – in a team environment, you must certainly be supportive of your teammates, but never hold yourself responsible for your friend's successes or failures. They are not yours to deal with. Also, in the fierce competition that prevails, you must be eternally vigilant of your words and deeds, as these can always be turned around and held against you.

THE BEGINNING OF CHANGE

Things began to change slowly when Mr Makarand Waingankar[23] first began to work with me and then later introduced me to Dr Kinjal Suratwala (who I've mentioned earlier). From there my journey from minus to zero began. I met a series of guides and coaches including Mr Rajshekar, Mr Abey Kuruvilla and finally my spiritual teacher Sri M.

4. The role of a coach

JIDDU KRISHNAMURTI, the world-famous philosopher, had this to say about the role of a teacher:[24]

> What is a teacher? It is the greatest profession in the world, though the least respected, for if he is deeply and seriously concerned the teacher is bringing about the un-conditioning of the human brain. Not only his own, but also that of the student. He is conditioned and the student is conditioned, whether he admits it or not, this is a fact. And in a relationship with the student he is helping both the student and himself to free consciousness from limitation.[25]

On this process of freeing a student from limitation, I would like to share a short story my first cricket coach, Shankar Sir,[26] once told me. The story segues into this chapter, which talks about the important role that coaches play in shaping the destiny of a player.

THE STORY OF THE SHEEP-LION

A heavily pregnant lioness was going about the jungle in search of prey. Seeing a flock of sheep, she jumped upon them giving birth in the process but dying in the effort. A healthy baby lion was born, motherless. It was raised by the sheep. It grew up with them, ate grass, and bleated like them. And though in time it became a full-grown lion, it thought it was a sheep.

Some time later, another lion came in search of prey. It was astonished to find that in the midst of this flock of sheep was a lion, fleeing like the sheep at the advance of danger. The lion tried to get near the sheep-lion and tell him that he was not a sheep but a lion, but the poor animal ran away. The lion waited for his opportunity and one day found the sheep-lion sleeping. He approached him and said, "Listen, you are a lion." "No, I am a sheep," replied the sheep-lion in fear, trained as his mind was in that belief.

The lion tried again but the sheep-lion refused to believe him. Frustrated, the lion dragged the sheep-lion to a lake and said, "Look here mate, here is my reflection and there is yours, decide for yourself." The sheep-lion looked at both their reflections and the knowledge suddenly dawned – I am and always was a lion. On discovering his true identity, he roared ferociously and fearlessly. The bleating was gone. Comprehending his real nature, he was born again, leaving behind his sheepish life, entering a new world of power and grandeur.

Similarly, under the spell of a multitude of factors, our minds suffer from 'sheepish' tendencies. Society shapes impressionable minds to meet its demands. The acquired values, ideas and beliefs combine to inhibit our inner lion. It's the same way by which immensely powerful elephants are falsely conditioned by mahouts to believe they cannot break free from a piddly little chain nailed to the ground.

The question is, how do you unbridle your inner lion and live a free, fearless and fulfilling life true to your potential? I believe the answer most times is in finding a good teacher. A teacher, if he indeed is deeply and seriously concerned, will bring about this awakening of the inner lion in his pupil.

How and where does one find such a teacher? Just as the wheel of fortune turned for the sheep-lion when he encountered a caring and wise fellow-lion, "rest assured", say the masters for, "when the student is ready, the teacher will appear."

THE IMPORTANCE OF A TEACHER

While we are without doubt eventually responsible for our own thoughts, words and deeds, it cannot be denied that a teacher plays a vital role in our development. Going back in time, we know the crucial part that Chanakya played in the rise of Emperor Chandragupta Maurya and the glorious Mauryan Empire. Chanakya was often referred to as a kingmaker.

In the same way, coaches can either be kingmakers or sheepmakers. Sachin Tendulkar often speaks of the role his childhood coach, Ramakant Achrekar, played in shaping his game and life.

Professional sport is a highly pressurised cauldron. Players are always being tested. In such an environment, the proverb 'one performance doesn't make a summer' holds true. Our examinations happen in an arena in the full glare of the public eye, with the accompanying stresses and anxieties.

High expectations and fierce competition (at all levels) often kill the joy of playing. The fear of failure becomes the prime motivating energy which in turn has a crippling effect on performance. For most players, the path to the pinnacle of their sport is filled with such apprehensions and insecurities.

Adding to all that, we have to handle academics. Education cannot be ignored while we wait for the promise of a livelihood from sport. Since professional sport is demanding in terms of time, mind and body, juggling both sports and studies is a great challenge. To meet this challenge, various necessary habits and qualities need to be developed.

Hence the relationship a player shares with his coach, mentor, parent and administrator is critical to how he undertakes this journey. Skilled teachers can guide a player in areas such as time management, nutrition, mental/physical training and people management. These challenges pose formidable obstacles to a player's growth and performance, if not handled correctly.

Unfortunately, while there are examinations to certify coaches, not everyone who passes these exams is an enlightened coach. This can result in devastating outcomes for a player.

The ugly side of sports: Vampire coaches

Like in politics, sport has its share of powerful people such as coaches and selectors, who have our careers in the palm of their hands. Of course, not all of them are bad. In fact, most of them are well meaning and genuinely motivated to do the best possible job in trying circumstances. But unfortunately, a few bad apples can have a disproportionately negative impact on the minds and careers of players.

I want to share a story that Mr Rajesh Kamath[27] told me. The pavilion in Bengaluru's Chinnaswamy stadium is located on what can be called a first floor. A player walks down a flight of stairs and through a narrow pathway that leads to the field of play. On the left of the pathway there is seating for spectators.

As Mr Kamath walked out to open the batting, he heard a voice call out to him from the spectators' area. It was the voice of a selector who yelled out, "If you do not score a hundred, pack your bags and go back to Dharwad (Mr Kamath's hometown)." Well, Mr Kamath made a century.

I asked him, "You mean to say the added pressure helped you perform?"

"Of course not!" he replied. "It was like my mind was bombed and I hardly saw the first few balls, anything could have happened. But then I buckled down and began to concentrate."

Coaches can either make the journey hard for a player or help it greatly. How can he make things worse? By saying things like:

- "If you want to play a higher level of cricket, you better perform now. I don't care how you do it, otherwise all the hard work goes to waste and once you pass a certain age you will feel like a loser all your life."
- "If you don't score, you won't find a place in the next game, because X is performing really well these days and may take your place."
- "There is no hope for you, give up cricket."

When coaches speak this way, it is most demoralising. I've often questioned myself about this negative approach:

- Are coaches not making one fearful of consequences, when in fact one should be made fearless?
- Are they not shaping one's thinking using fear?
- Are they inculcating a result oriented and not a process-oriented approach?

So a coach can make life miserable by evaluating a player on the basis of result alone, discounting all other factors that influence performance. I know of many coaches whose moods are directly proportional to the team's performance. They are fun to be around only when their team has done well. And that is how they condition you to look at success and failure: "Be happy only if you have a performance to justify it, otherwise sit in a corner and sulk."

This is the kind of pressure one is constantly subjected to. Instruction is always conveyed with a threat built into it. Fearful scenarios are intentionally introduced, because coaches seem convinced that it is the best way to extract conformity and performance. When our root relationships – the ones we share with our parents, teachers, or mentors – are based on fear, what then will be the plight of the subsequent relationships we enter into?

Coming back to the pressure I described in the introduction chapter, board exams are built up for years as this big life-changing event. It is projected as the most important examination of our lives and gives us the sense that life ends if we fare poorly. Hence, these exams are more feared than anticipated. There is no way learning can be fun in such an atmosphere and when you learn out of fear, you are always anxious. Besides, *how long can one carry fearful feelings and function normally?*

That fateful exam night, when failure became a real possibility, it was as though a bullet pierced the tightly packed baggage of expectation in my mind. Out came all the worms of negative thoughts and emotions against which I was powerless.

Some coaches inject an overdose of fearful perspectives. Over time all these perspectives cause impressions that build up below the surface. Most players are constantly haunted by the fears of failing, being replaced, being looked down upon, or of not realising their full potential. The reasons for fear are plenty, and we all have our individual mechanisms to deal with it. But almost always, the fear is felt and then temporarily overcome. *Wild celebration upon success is only the celebration of the momentary relief from fear and worry rather than a sense of accomplishment.* It is as if you are vindicated after being put on trial.

The psychological impact of such coaches

Ultimately, fear hides the truth. When a player is fearful, will he not find it hard to open up to those who are supposed to support him? When he isn't speaking or sharing, the truth will always be hidden, isn't it?

Perhaps powerful people don't really care to know or understand. Often the rhetoric officials use for placing that kind of pressure is, "We are making them tough," or "Only if you put pressure will they perform," or "This level of the game is all about handling pressure," and more humbug of that kind.

An official once offered this as justification: "In India because of the sheer number of cricketers, it is elimination that takes place and not selection." All these explanations are dubious at best. I wonder if these people even realise the amount of pressure there already is. The last thing anybody needs is an overdose. A sincere player obviously wants to do well himself, and has his own pressures to handle. A little sensitivity never hurt anybody.

My friends and contemporaries at the first class level confirm that coaches sometimes manipulate players on purpose, because of politics or personal prejudices to further their own careers. When coaches, administrators or selectors are partial, it becomes extremely difficult for the player who feels discriminated against.

Elimination as a policy

In the recently concluded Ranji trophy, the Karnataka team that dominated the season was celebrating winning the treble[28] for the first time ever. But there was one man who was not so jubilant. Mentally exhausted, he did the unthinkable. Although only 25 years old, he decided to break all ties and bring a premature end to a 14-year partnership with a cricket association he adored.

It begs the question, what made him do this? Especially when it seemed that all was going well for him? For only a month earlier, in his comeback game, which happened to be the final of the Ranji Trophy, he had made a century. I remember opening the paper to find a picture of him with a raised bat and broad smile, and thinking, "Wow, this guy just doesn't give in" and "Nothing is permanent, how easily fortunes change in this game." A month and a few games later, he was dropped from the side once again.

After talking to him it emerged that he was 'the chosen one'- chosen for elimination in this case. Obviously the player does not want to be named. But he told me that for two years he played the game with an axe over his head, and repeatedly rescued himself. This entire process exhausted him, sucking dry the joy and love he had for the game. He elaborated:

> Everyone told me that I have to be tough, handle the pressure and fight back and so I did, I even scored a double hundred. A couple of games later I found myself out of the playing eleven and subsequently was not even a part of the one-day side. I have never heard of someone being dropped only a few innings after scoring a double hundred. They were looking for me to fail, it was clear. I felt helpless and I desperately sought an explanation.

He said he tried calling the selectors but they seemed more interested in deflecting blame. None offered an explanation. He continued, "It hurt me immeasurably to know that as ex-captain only a few seasons ago, why was I not extended the basic courtesy of an explanation? I wanted to know if there were some valid cricketing reasons to justify my ouster."

I replied saying competition for spots in the team was fierce, talented youngsters were coming through the ranks, and the team had won in all formats. He retorted, "I was an integral part of that success, and I understand I am not indispensable. If I don't perform please drop me, and in any case if performance was a factor, the selectors would have been the first to point that out."

Right or wrong, he decided he was not going to play in an environment so hostile and apathetic. He also decided that he was not the association's play toy, and refused to allow himself to be treated shabbily. He might as well take a stand and quit (not from the game, but from the association) on his own terms, as dignity and self-respect still mattered to him. Many players don't do this, as it is considered weak. So they turn up and silently suffer, before gradually fading away.

I too have played under some coaches who are plain sadists and pose a real danger to naïve, pliable minds. Almost all coaches at the state level are ex first-class players themselves, with so-called illustrious careers to their names. I remember one person in particular who was infamous for giving players a harrowing time. He seemed more interested in talking-up his generation and its achievements, while always looking down at us. He had a superiority complex that was suffocating and he certainly didn't believe that, "Appreciation is a basic human need."

Far worse, he was sectarian in every level of this thinking, and judged people on the basis of their ethnic or linguistic background. He once told me, out of the blue, during a match, "You have given up the fight for a separate land because coffee prices have fallen, isn't it?" And he was not joking.

It was an unnecessary provocation and he has likewise provoked several other players. Instead of performing the sacred work of coaching, he often fought with players. I have not met anyone who is so unanimously disliked by the entire cricketing population of a state.

Ironically, this coach had taken and passed the highest level of coaching certification in the country. The point here is that education and certification did not change his basic values in any way. He came out with the same prejudices, but his enhanced technical knowledge was deemed good enough to unleash him on unsuspecting youngsters.

This is an indictment of the coaching syllabus itself, which seems to lack a mechanism that evaluates coaches on human parameters such as bias, sensitivity, humility, understanding, love and so on.

It is not always the coaches who behave badly. Administrators can be cruel in their own way. Another friend of mine, a first-class cricketer, related a shocking incident. He had injured his finger while playing and was advised surgery by a doctor. Contracted players are entitled to medical expenses and hence he approached an administrator for the necessary authorisation.

The official commanded, "Show me your injury." My friend's finger was heavily bandaged so he proceeded to gently remove the bandage. The official rudely said, "I don't have all day for you," and yanked off the bandage without showing any consideration.

Clearly, this is shocking and unacceptable behaviour. First, the official didn't trust the player and second, despite common sense knowledge that injuries should be treated with care, he caused more damage. This official is a famous name, and society venerates some of these men of position and influence.

But players are frightened of these very same people and do not dare speak up. Of course, there are good administrators too – but they too suffer from the same fears that players do. Their jobs are at stake and it doesn't seem worth the effort to jeopardise their future for 'small' players.

An intelligent and mature sportsman will pick up his bags and run as far as possible from such grandly certified coaches and powerful administrators. But in most cases, running away is not an option. To survive such an environment, only a player who can insulate himself can succeed. Given that we play the game from a very early age, we do not have the maturity to deal with bad behaviour from the powers-that-be.

The only way for players to handle this is to become thick skinned, but then there's always an undercurrent of anger lurking. This fury manifests itself in foul-mouthed celebrations when milestones such as a century are reached. And then retired cricketers providing commentary ask, "Why aren't these youngsters happy when they do well? Why are they looking angry?"

In contrast to vampire coaches, there are others who I call 'impact coaches' and 'impact parents'. They are the exact opposite. I'll talk about impact coaches first.

Impact coaches

In cricket, there's a term called 'impact player' that refers to someone who can single-handedly turn a game on its head. Likewise, there are 'impact coaches' or mentors, who genuinely care about players and profoundly impact their lives.

The contrast between this category of people and the ones I spoke about earlier is in the language they speak and the way they treat you. They are understanding, compassionate, sensitive, purposeful, patient, wise and selfless. The overwhelming message I got from almost all of them was:

> What's most important is that you enjoy what you are doing and give your best. Do not worry about anything else. We are proud of you either way, success or failure. However, we will pull you up if you are lazy and don't give a 100%.

These statements again place emphasis on *process, effort and intention*. When effectively communicated, it gets the player thinking about how to have fun and enjoy in all situations. This takes away the entire burden that comes with obsessing over the result.

Instruction or suggestion can make a positive or negative impression on a player's mind. Below are a few questions a coach could ask of himself:

- What is best for the player?
- What kind of instruction is healthy for the player and likely to make him fearless?
- How to be approachable so the player is able to share without embarrassment or remorse his bad days, as easily as he does his good ones?
- How to create a relationship based on trust?
- Should a coach promote obsession with result or cultivate love for meaningful activity?

From personal experience I can say that only when a coach or anybody else earned my trust would I open up to him. Once trusted, he could even scream at me when needed, and I wouldn't take it personally for I knew the coach had my best interests at heart.

In my stint as coach at the Peepal Grove School,[29] I learnt that if approached with the right spirit, coaching can be a very enriching experience. Children can ask thought-provoking questions and hold a mirror to your face.

Life has taught me the hard way that motive, intent and preparation are the only factors one can control to some degree. By controlling these, we greatly increase our chances of success. But there is still no guarantee, as there is no predictable link between effort and success (this is explained in greater detail in the chapter on goal setting).

The coach and the player must work together to identify barriers, study the conditions from which they emerge and resolve them. This can only be done in an environment of mutual trust and friendship. I fully agree with what Sachin Tendulkar said – that a coach should be a friend.[30] I know this is easier said than done, but it is very important.

Yes, impact coaches do exist and I have been lucky to have worked with a few of them. You may not hear about them because they often work in the background. An impact coach need not be heard or seen but is definitely felt.

ABEY KURUVILLA – AN IMPACT COACH

Mr Kuruvilla is the most unconventional teacher I have come across. I have seen him from close quarters in his roles as selector, manager, player, director and coach at DYPSA. (Although he has written the foreword to this book, please take my word that I have not been influenced in any way to write this section.)

When a match is in progress, he keenly observes proceedings sitting away from the dressing room. If he feels the boys have given their 100%, he congratulates them regardless of the result. As a coach he has never called for team meetings based on outcome. I will give you several instances.

We once lost the Times Shield 'B' division semi-final after gaining the first innings lead. I really thought Mr Kuruvilla would tear into us that day. But all he said to us in the two-minute post-match meeting was, "Well played boys, cricket mein ek team harta hai aur ek team jeeththa hai" ("in cricket, one team wins and the other loses"). We had really tried hard right through the game and he had seen that.

A year earlier, in the Times Shield 'C' division finals, I played what was the closest match of my life. After we scored 456 (I made 80), the opposition were 350 odd with three wickets down in reply, and looking really good to chase down our target. Everyone was anxious and I have never seen Mr Kuruvilla pace around the ground as much as he did that day. Mr Vijay Patil, President of the D Y Patil Group, took time off his busy schedule to watch that game. That's how much cricket means to them, and such was the management's desire to see us promoted to 'B' division.

There was a tangible nervous tension on both sides, when our hard working fast bowler got the edge of a well-set batsman. The catch came straight to me and I made a mess of it to say the least. From that moment, my mind went off on a guilt expedition because I thought I had put down the trophy.

At tea, I assumed the team (especially me) would get a mouthful from Mr Kuruvilla. But he was restrained as ever and understood how tense we already were. He's only human and I'm sure he was anxious himself, but he never pushed that anxiety onto us. Neither did Mr Patil; I found him to have the real sportsman spirit. He accepted all outcomes gracefully and I never saw him interfere in team affairs.

After tea, on our way back out, Mr Kuruvilla patted me on the back and said, "Come on now, one final effort, let's see if they break." And break they did, for within the first three overs after tea, three wickets fell in the most dramatic 12 deliveries I have witnessed. Pravin Tambe (our captain) wanted a change of end and handed the ball to Rohit Rane,[31] who proceeded to pick up three wickets in two overs, including the batsman whose catch I dropped. I was obviously most relieved and we eventually won the game by around 30 runs.

After the final wicket fell, the whole team gathered in a huddle and began jumping in celebration. Mr Patil gleefully ran onto the ground like a child full of energy and at that moment, I understood the meaning of the term 'team-sport.'

The victory was such a relief that I broke down, only to be consoled by Mr Kuruvilla who said, "No one would have blamed you if we had lost." I wanted to correct him saying mine were tears of joy, but I let it be. During the after-match celebration, Mr Patil announced a cash reward to all players and said, "I always knew there was something about this team," to which Mr Kuruvilla replied, "It's their team spirit."

Mr Kuruvilla had said that our strength is not that we have the best individual players, but that we combine well as a team. That core group of Pravin Tambe, Kumar Subramaniam, Yogesh Pawar, Abey Wagmare, Ashok Kadam (as coach) and myself were consistently part of the side that won three championships in six seasons and in all divisions of Times Shield (A, B and C).

The last instance I want to cite was during the first year of our Times Shield 'A' division match. We were 45 for six and the opposition's quartet of pacers, all first class bowlers, had wreaked havoc on our batting. While all this was happening out in the field, in the pavilion there was music blaring from a player's system, and no one bothered turning down the volume.

Mr Kuruvilla entered the pavilion and most of us expected an angry remark of, "Turn off the music and focus on the game" or something like that. But all he said was, "Kaun sa gaana hai, gaana change karo na" ("which song is this, please change the song"). And then he proceeded to say, "Woh log mast dal raha hai na" ("those guys are really bowling well isn't it?"). We were all most surprised, conditioned as we were to expect 'scoldings' (as a schoolboy would say) when we failed.

I am sure India is filled with many such stories; great stories don't just happen at the international level alone! That feeling of family, of belonging, the drawing together of people across backgrounds and focusing their energies towards a common cause, is a true test of any leader. To promote that cordial environment and camaraderie among the players was made possible only on account of the loving personalities and leadership qualities of both Mr Patil and Mr Kuruvilla.

All these incidents clearly indicated to me that they were truly appreciative of the various factors that intermingle to make a desired result possible. And hence all they could do was to judge a team's performance on the basis of their collective effort and intent.

I have often heard Mr Kuruvilla praise players saying, "He always gives a hundred per cent on the field." Every time he pointed out flaws or weaknesses in my game, he did so by first reinforcing my strengths before telling me how I could improve. In contrast, *vampire coaches are like flies who look for the ulcer while impact coaches are bees that look for the honey in the flower.*

Earnest striving is more important to Mr Kuruvilla than anything else. In the eight seasons that I played in Mumbai, I can remember only one instance when he admonished the team. This was in a Mahindra Shield game, when we meekly surrendered and lost despite being the stronger side.

Being reserved by nature, Mr Kuruvilla never spoke much, but when he did, it was always direct and to the point; short sentences loaded with meaning. We deserved his strong words.

He constantly stressed how important the mental side of the game was. In one game, I twisted my ankle badly – it was black and blue. But he told me that evening, "You must bat tomorrow, I don't want to hear about the pain." I could not say anything because I had seen him batting with an injury earlier that season. He scored a half-century playing with a sprained, bandaged hand. He would also say, "Good form and bad form are all in the head." I ultimately did learn that all faults do lie within one's own mind.

I suspect he does not believe much in team meetings because he prefers speaking to players individually. He understands that the one-size fits all approach does not work. Of his coaching philosophy, he says:

> You must know what to say to whom and when. Here again timing is all-important. You cannot talk to everyone the same way. There are some who are exceptionally gifted but very lazy. There are some who are above average, some below average. There are some who work extremely hard and don't know how to relax. There are some who need emotional support. There are some who need technical support and so on. Players have various work ethics, tendencies and styles. Therefore, you cannot give the same advice or suggestion to everyone.
>
> Some lack even the basic talent and they must be told so. Their talent probably lies elsewhere. This does not mean they should stop playing. They can be encouraged to play the game for fun but must be cleverly cautioned against nursing serious ambitions. To them, you must not sell dreams or raise their expectation, for in trying to meet them they end up mentally troubling themselves. This does not mean there isn't the proverbial 'lion' in them, of course there is, and when directed to a profession where their talent lies, it will come out.

Albert Einstein had summed it up perfectly when he said: "Everybody is a genius. But if you judge a fish by its ability to climb a tree, it will live its entire life believing it is stupid."[32]

Mr Kuruvilla holds several important positions. As such, he has players calling on him all the time (I was one of them), coaxing him for a chance to play one tournament or another. Though most humble, friendly and approachable, he always maintained objectivity.

There is a saying in the Arthashastras of Chanakya: "The king, severe with the rod, becomes a terror for beings. The king, mild with the rod, is despised. The king, just with the rod, is honoured."[33]

The above description fits Mr Kuruvilla perfectly. He has both a soft and a tough side. During match days, if it happened to be any player's birthday, he would have a cake brought to the pavilion; during tea-time a cake-cutting event would be held.

Most of all, he acts as a huge tree, whose generous shade has sheltered and mentored many a career to fruition. All in all, I'd like to thank Mr Kuruvilla wholeheartedly for teaching me what it means to be a professional.

But while good coaches like Mr Kuruvilla can boost you up, hard-driving parents can crush your spirit.

Vampire parents

Parents and immediate family are your first, natural coaches. But they too frequently promote a mindset that is fixated on reward and a 'win at all costs' attitude. This is because they are also subjected to the same result-oriented values of society. In contrast, what's required are 'impact parents.'

Impact parents

What attitude should parents have with regard to their child's sporting career? Let's see what the 'God of cricket' has to say. Just as I started writing this chapter, Sachin Tendulkar's illustrious career came to a close. In the press conference post his retirement, he was asked a couple of questions: first, about his family's reaction to his performances over the years. And second, about his son Arjun's cricketing career.

Tendulkar's responses to both questions are revealing. Let's begin with his family's reaction:

> The beauty of my family is that they never lost balance. Whether I scored a hundred or 15, 20 it didn't matter. My father and mother always had encouraging words for me. I was able to perform well since my school days because the balance was maintained at home. Nobody got carried away with my good performances and celebrated those occasions endlessly. Like any other Indian family we used to buy a packet of sweets and offer those sweets to the Almighty and thank the Almighty for everything that is happening in my

life. And that process continued, even yesterday my mother told me when I spoke to her later on, that I have kept sweets in front of God, and that continues, it will never stop.

Their reaction to me when I got back from any tour was never related to the way I performed, it was more about parents and their child and it has always stayed that way.

On his attitude towards his son's cricket (translated from Hindi):

As a father, I would like to tell you all (the media) to leave him alone. Let him enjoy the game, don't place expectations on him every time, saying his father used to perform in a certain way and so also should Arjun.

If I had that kind of pressure then perhaps, I would have a pen in my hand and not a cricket bat, because my father was a professor in the field of literature. However, at that time, no one questioned my father as to why there was a bat in my hand and not a pen. So I want to say this, that Arjun has chosen to hold a bat in his hand and when it comes to cricket he is most passionate.

You must be madly in love with the sport to bring the best out of you. He [Arjun] is madly in love with cricket and that is what matters. Performance ho na ho mein pressure nahi dalna chahta uske upar aur aapko bhi nahi dalna chahiye (whether he performs or not, I don't put any pressure on him and I don't think you should too). Koi bhi player, usko aap khula chhod do, he is able to perform better, and above all he is able to enjoy cricket (whoever the player, if you let him be free he is able to perform better). And that is what I expect. He has to just enjoy cricket. Aagey ka jo script rahega, woh uparwala decide karta hai, hum koi nahi kartey (beyond this, an individual's destiny is decided by the Almighty, not by any of us).[34]

It is obvious that in addition to Tendulkar's natural abilities, it is his upbringing and the unseen environment his family created that was responsible for his phenomenal and sustained success. While his family did this naturally, it can be labelled as a process oriented approach that got the best out of him. Unfortunately, cricket and other sports are littered with the careers of sportsmen and women who have not had similar, stable and balanced home environments.

If a player feels accepted and loved only when he achieves a particular result, he is bound to fear failure. When we apply ourselves to any task under such pressure, the process is driven by anxious thought. And fearful action is impotent.

Positive parenting can be applied in any sphere of life. One of my friends has a son who wrongly spelt a four letter word in a junior school test. The child was upset that he couldn't even spell a small word correctly. While my friend doesn't really care about marks or grades, he wanted his son to gain confidence and be free of the fear that he can't spell. To do this he decided to teach the child how to spell the longest English word, pneumonoultramicroscopicsilicovolcanoconiosis. This is an apparently artificially created word meaning a lung disease caused by the inhalation of very fine ash and sand dust.[35] My friend told his son very lovingly that if you can learn how to spell the longest word, every other word will become simple, thereby removing the mental block. The child thought his father had gone bonkers.

My friend taught his son the simple technique of breaking up a long word into smaller chunks. It took a bit of work, but once the child learned the longest word, all fear of spelling evaporated. Thereafter, he enthusiastically began spelling out the word to anyone who happened to be around.

In this context, the word itself is not important. The aim was not just to teach the spelling of the longest word. The objective was to give the child reassurance and confidence. In short, the attitude of the parent was constructive rather than destructive.

The ideal coach

Ultimately, a coach must have insight, a good brain and a big heart. A coach does not become great by working with a few already established players, and then using their recommendations to grow his clientele. A coach should make an average player great, by expanding the horizon of his pupil and showing him his proper place in the game. *He must prepare the player not just for the game of his choice, but also to win the larger and more important game of life.*

Success in any field is about knowing the 'why and how' of things. Successful people know why things work a certain way and that's what allows them to succeed. Therefore the role of an educator is to provide inputs about technical, tactical, physical, emotional and if need be even spiritual needs.

Such a person must himself possess the knowledge, experience and expertise required to deliver insights on the finer aspects of the subject. It's a tall order for one person to possess all these qualities. But at the very minimum, the coach should be aware of his own limitations and acknowledge them.

I will take a moment to explain what I mean, growing up and being coached in various clinics over a period of 10 years. I have often heard coaches say the following three things:

- Keep things simple
- Enjoy the game
- Be in the present

Such advice was often given with an attitude of superiority. Seldom would coaches ever go beyond these phrases to explain exactly what they meant. I would constantly succumb to the same pressures and was unable to keep things simple, enjoy myself, or be in the present. Theories and solutions people offered only led to new problems that returned to slap me on the face.

The ages between 18 and 22 are a critical phase for a sportsperson to make the leap into the big league, and success depends on his ability to execute the above three points. It's far more difficult than it sounds. Sometimes, to arrive at simplicity, it requires a complex process for which a teacher is essential. Once you find that simplicity you become independent, which is the culmination of all learning.

The coach also has the challenging task of assessing whether the student is ready to receive instructions. Due to overload of information nowadays, most coaches have some technical advice to offer. Do the cricketers need so much advice? This is the question to be asked. Juniors are so habituated to advice that if a coach does not point a technical fault for a week or so, he assumes either the coach is not interested or knows little about coaching. Suggestions and advice are given at a drop of a hat, leaving the boys confused.

The intelligent ones are the most vulnerable because they are smart enough to try out everything. Many cricketers are terrified of the 'T' word, 'Technique.' They just want to break the shackles of technique and play. Technique is essential, but the timing of the advice, i.e. when and where is even more important.

The right advice at the right time can turn one's game around in a matter of days. However, we as sportspeople should not place the entire responsibility on one person. We must also seek out coaches for our all-round development – I talk more of this in the chapter called, 'The Syncing of the Goliaths.'

CONCLUSION: A SUGGESTION FOR REFORM

It would be great if selectors, coaches and administrators are asked to sign a code of conduct declaring that they will not be sectarian, and be free of any other similar prejudices.

I would like to end this chapter the way I began, with a quote from Jiddu Krishnamurti:

> Are you going to be thrown into this world of strife, confusion, war, hatred? Are you going to conform, fit in, and accept all the old values? You know what these values are – money, position, prestige and power. That is all man wants and society wants you to fit into that pattern of values. But if you now begin to think, to observe, to learn, not from books, but to learn for yourself by watching, listening to everything that is happening around you, you will grow up to be a different human being – one who cares, who has affection, who loves people. Perhaps if you live that way, you might find a truly religious life.[36]

5. The accidental 'zone' experience

BEFORE WE PROCEED I would like to outline what the 'zone' means in sporting parlance. It was popularised by psychologist Mihaly Csikszentmihalyi in his book *Flow: The Psychology of Optimal Experience*. Here's his description of 'flow':

> There's this focus that, once it becomes intense, leads to a sense of ecstasy, a sense of clarity: you know exactly what you want to do from one moment to the other; you get immediate feedback. You know that what you need to do is possible to do, even though difficult, and sense of time disappears, you forget yourself, you feel part of something larger. And once the conditions are present, what you are doing becomes worth doing for its own sake.[37]

I have certainly experienced this state a few times in my career, as I am sure most sportsmen have. I want to relate my first such experience, as it was a career saving and watershed moment for me.

It happened when I was 22 and not yet a first class cricketer like I had hoped to be. The issue of age had started caving in on me. Everyone told me that I had missed the bus and it was time for me to move on with life. I was only 22!

That year I had trained especially hard during the lead up to the season because I wanted to impress my new club, BUCC (Bengaluru United Cricket Club). Three games into the season, I had repeatedly failed with both bat and gloves (conceding 32 byes in one game). I was thoroughly disgusted and wanted to quit. A senior player even advised me to stop playing cricket. It really hurt because I had no other plan in life.

All these factors collectively made that period a very hard time. My confidence was low, my mind was negative and I found it extremely hard to smile. I constantly worried that I would get dropped from the side, and imagined how embarrassing it would be for me to face people sitting on the sidelines.

It felt like a good performance was years away. The team was packed with the state's top players, all of whom I was very eager to impress. I was extremely disappointed that I had done quite the opposite. Soon after, I stumbled on the most unbelievable batting experience of my life.

THE OPTIMAL PERFORMANCE STATE

After my failures, I was pushed down the batting order and the gloves were taken away from me, rightly so. A 14-year-old was made the keeper and sent ahead of me in the batting line-up. I felt insulted and brooded over these developments the entire day.

As far as I was concerned, all my cricketing dreams were over. *I decided to quit*; I could no longer breathe the air of shame and humiliation that comes with underperforming. After the first day's play, I went home thoroughly exhausted from a bruised ego. I hit the bed at 7pm and woke up the next morning with a splitting headache and high temperature. That's when I learnt first-hand how mind and body are connected. All the mental negativity had pulled my body down.

I reached towards my phone to call my captain and inform him that I would not be able to play. Just as I was about to call, the phone rang. It was my mother. I told her of my condition and she said, "Don't worry, just go and play this match, whatever happens we will support you. If you put this kind of effort in any other field you will become a king." I also spoke to dad and he said, "Please continue playing." These words dissuaded me from calling my captain, and I proceeded to the ground with a heavy head and high temperature.

At the ground, day two began with us declaring with the score around 350; I hadn't batted. We took the field and I had a shabby day, fielding some and misfielding some more. Our bowlers regularly picked up wickets and soon the opposition was 240 odd for eight. By then the afternoon sun was out and my condition worsened. I requested my captain for permission to leave the field assuming he would readily agree. But he surprisingly told me, "You should never leave the field, no matter what," and I reluctantly complied.

In hindsight I am glad he said what he did, because soon after we bowled the opposition out and were left with 30 overs to bat. Our manager walked up to me and asked, "Will you open the batting as you never got to bat in the first innings?" I readily agreed and thanked him. While padding up to go in, I vividly remember telling myself, "Just go down fighting, anyhow you are going to quit after this game."

I walked out and took guard. What followed in the next one and half hours of batting is something for which I don't have a convincing explanation to this day. I hit long sixes, crisp boundaries and batted just the way I always dreamt. For the first time in my life, every ball hit the meat of my bat.

I made 92 off 60 odd balls and I don't know how. I reached 50 in 27 deliveries and remember the umpire telling me, "That was quick." The bowling attack was no pushover; all the bowlers had at some point played for junior state, and the wicket was no belter.

I felt a strange *stillness* overcome my mind and the incessant mental chatter was missing. The small cricket ball seemed twice its size and the centre of my bat was everywhere. Every ball felt like a donkey drop and I had plenty of time to play it. My footwork was precise and my shot selection effortless. The bowler was irrelevant – I gave importance only to the ball. It was the most perfectly orchestrated innings of my life.

I remember hitting three boundaries in the first over itself. A senior player walked across the ground cheering me on, slowly joined by my other teammates. It was a huge compliment and they positioned themselves behind the sightscreen to get a better view of my innings.

I had no clue how it all happened because my physical and mental signs were to the contrary. I say 'it' because the state 'I' was in, 'it' could not have been me. Where did 'it' come from then?

Also, at that stage in my life I had no faith in God or myself. I was a complete atheist and Lance Armstrong heavily influenced my personality and ideas. In his book *It's Not About The Bike*' he stresses on hard work and sincerity, not so much on God. Armstrong's comeback story was so phenomenal and inspirational that I adopted his views, only to find out years later that he had been cheating (what a let down!).[38]

Retrospective analysis

When I look back at my performance that day, I was initially in a state of utter hopelessness. There was no expectation whatsoever, no lusting for fame, no fear of failing, no pressure of ambition, nobody to impress or prove a point to, nobody to beat or compete against. I didn't feel like I had to get anywhere. There was no fear of being judged, no desperation to obtain a particular result, to look good, there were no thoughts of the future or the past, no concern about technique or a player's sledge. By force of circumstance I let go of all agenda and slipped into present moment.

Funny thing is, just before I was dismissed on 92 I had thought, "Oh If I make a hundred here, it will be my team's first century this season." When that thought entered my mind, it was all over. Till that point I was absorbed in the present. I was in the 'zone,' and the whole experience had happened by accident.

In other words, when my mind was free of the usual programs, it allowed my inherent talent and skills to rise to the surface. My potential that was otherwise *captive to the constant mental gossip was momentarily unleashed*. So I just went out there and batted.

After that exhilarating experience, I gave up all thoughts and ideas of quitting, and still continue to play. But all those mental conditions did return as they had only vanished temporarily. Nonetheless, from that day on I always believed that 'anything can happen' and that I indeed had access to another gear. I thank the game for this understanding.

It was also the first time I felt the presence of something other than my mind. The presence offered hope, it was trying to tell me something, signalling me to "Play on." Had it not been for that knock, I would have missed out on the wonderful Mumbai and D Y Patil experiences that proved to be a huge learning curve. Like everything in life, once you've tasted the best, you cannot settle for anything else. I had fluked an ideal state and being an idealist, I wished to stumble upon it again and again.

I could not help but think, "If I can do it once, why not every time." And thus rejuvenated, I began a personal journey to discover a method to intentionally access that state. I wanted to imbibe the qualities necessary for my mind to enter and stay absorbed in the present. I thought if I played from that state, no one could come close to me. I later found that to be a tall order, because the mind is tricky, easily stunned by the objective world and distracted away from the present.

While batting or keeping I still found it hard to replicate the mind that allowed the knock to happen. I thought having experienced it once, it would come back easily, but I was wrong. In some ways, that innings restored all my old ambitions and thinking that were absent during the knock. The habitual programs returned. While I now knew that I had another gear, my inability to access it on demand frustrated me.

THE STRUGGLE CONTINUES

People always cautioned me against 'thinking too much.' But with time I found myself wanting to know how to completely insulate my mind, once and for all, from all the negativity and pressure. I was fed-up of this constant struggle to stay positive and in the present. It had to come more naturally. I had no choice but to get to the root of the problem.

As I was to learn later, high states of mind are free of desperation and obsession. A mind that is devoted to the present is free of expectation and detached from reward. And as we've seen, societal values are not very conducive to this mind. The dichotomy was that I needed to be *detached from a particular result to obtain it*; yet I found people appreciating and taking notice of me only when I produced the result.

I was desperate to succeed and so pursued every possible lead that offered deliverance. I attended all sorts of courses and seminars, spoke to various domain experts, read self-help books and attended personality development forums. Nothing worked.

At a motivational seminar I attended the speaker said, "You are whole, complete and perfect," without clarifying the remark. He just wanted everyone to believe what he said was true.

It is an idea which surely tempts me into believing it, but again it's the ego that gets tempted. Were I really whole, complete and perfect, why would I feel the need to go to a seminar on motivation?

Maybe the perfect state he spoke about is our original state; I had no defence against that notion. But to understand and believe it, didn't I have to first realise that state? I wondered if it was some sort of a joke to become whole, complete and perfect within three or five days.

Usually, learning in such courses only succeeds in furthering the ego and creates more baggage. I think it's because these solutions are often sophisticated thought processes. No matter how powerful a thought or thought process, it has its limitations.

Beyond a point, I found that each attempt in this direction always had the effect of an anaesthetic. It dulled the pain for a while by creating some motivation and excitement, but eventually the feelings would wear off. The same old mental condition would re-emerge. The courses never struck at the cause of the condition; they either treated the symptoms or simply piled your mind with another set of ideas, which in turn caused another set of problems.

Long story short, between 2006 and 2009, I was yet to find a method I could trust. I always strived for that perfect state when playing, but never quite found it. Looking back, it was a period of great learning. I found the psychological pressures we face are of a homogeneous nature i.e., the cause of their emergence is the same, save for minor differences.

6. The KPL season of 2009

IN 2009, Mr Brijesh Patel – the then Secretary of KSCA (Karnataka State Cricket Association) and among the best cricket administrators in the country, announced the creation of the Karnataka Premier League (KPL). KPL was to be fashioned along the lines of IPL with music, dance, celebrity ambassadors, promotional events, team launches, auctions, pre, mid and post-match interviews, et al. There was considerable attention generated. The launch event was so well covered by the state media that even my grandmother, who is around 80 years old and lives in a village in Kodagu (Coorg), was aware of every minute detail.

KPL was being billed as the tournament that could catapult one's career into the big league. Naturally the excitement of players soared to a fever pitch. Every cricketer in Karnataka woke up with dreams revived. There were some players who had even come back from retirement.

Parents and relatives called me to say, "This is a great opportunity, you must take it or else you will have only yourself to blame." So you can imagine that there was a lot riding on us and expectations were sky high. All eyes were on the players put up for auction.

I thought the tournament would be my moment of reckoning. The problem was that I had built up a lot of toxicity in the process of finding myself a KPL team. I assumed that because I had been picked for the prestigious Safi Darashah tournament that year, I would very easily find a place in one of the eight KPL teams.

Expectations and assumptive thinking

Oscar Wilde said, "When you assume, you make an ass out of you and me." And on expectation, here's a quote: "Expectation is the root of all heartache" (source unknown).

I experienced diverse forms of expectation. The expectation I had of myself, the expectation others had of me and finally the expectations I had of others.

Just before the auction, I had a troublesome tooth that was extracted and I went to Kodagu for a couple of days to recover. When I returned, I found myself without a team. In those two days, I later learned, teams were auctioned, coaches were picked, and players relentlessly hounded team owners for spots. More than 80% of player positions were already taken. Almost every cricketer I spoke to had found a team or had been approached by somebody.

As opposed to acting with the urgency of a man whose hair is on fire, I had been resting in Kodagu. My diary entry for 11 August 2009 reads: "The evening practice in the nets is when I realised how late I moved on the whole KPL thing. I never thought getting a team would be so hard."

I had taken my eyes off the ball and paid the price. Clearly, I had misread the situation. In retrospect, I felt I should have been out there doing PR (public relations) – talking and meeting coaches of various teams and attending selection matches. But I had felt that was below my dignity. My ego was at an all-time high because I thought I had done enough to get picked on merit; everybody else who had played Safi Darashah easily found a team.

I remember asking my club secretary, "Sir, do you think I must attend the selection matches considering that I have done well this season?" He replied, "Of course you should." The very thought of having to play selection games where any and everybody would come and play, or approaching people and asking them to pick me, was unbearable.

One of the KPL teams was co-owned by a man whose son was playing for my club, of which I was the vice-captain. With over 500 runs that year, I thought I had at least impressed the owner's son. I had also worked really hard on my wicket-keeping with improved results. But when he arrived on the ground and handed contracts to two other players and not to me, I felt humiliated.

I later spoke to him over the phone and with much difficulty asked him why he had not considered me. He avoided answering me directly, but the message was clear: it was an outright rejection that left me feeling miserable.

To make matters worse, the KPL team was to be managed and mentored by the very same club we played for that season. I naturally expected my club to push my case. When I spoke to my club secretary he said, "We are trying to get one wicket-keeper in the auction but if that does not happen, you are surely in."

Their bid for that particular player failed and yet I was not called. I was left in the lurch. Now, there is no right and wrong here. Often it happens that a player thinks he has done enough to be picked, but selectors have a different view. Both sides will give you equally convincing rationales, for and against their case. Here I am simply expressing how I felt at the time. I nurse no grudge whatsoever against anyone concerned.

For years, I kept getting embarrassed by my failures. Despite my best efforts to stay positive, subconsciously I never expected anything to go my way. Patterns had formed and gripped my mind and I allowed them to define me. I gave importance to all the thoughts that would form. But strangely, I kept hoping that one day my mind would change.

In the end, it wasn't my mind but my fate that changed. I received an offer to play for the Mysore Maharajas team, which I happily and gratefully accepted.

The frustrations of a passionate mind

The Mysore Maharajas team management made it very clear that I was not their first choice wicket-keeper. My arguments failed to persuade them to change their mind. Straightaway the first choice keeper in the Maharajas team became my nemesis, as he stood in the way of my progress. My thinking stooped to new lows. I secretly wished that he would mess up so I would get a chance.

I had gotten used to carrying all these insecurities and burdens, but I still managed to impress in the few practice matches we played. A few decent knocks with the bat and a brilliant down the leg stumping with the gloves, made me hope that I would make the playing XI in time for the first game. But that was not be, and I brooded.

Any little thing could pull me down since all my ideas of contentment were tied to success in cricket. My happiness rested on very fragile ground. Ultimately, it is happiness that leads to performance, not the other way around.

Normally, a day before a KPL match, it was customary to have practice nets during which the batting order mirrored the batting order for the match. I got to bat only towards the end of the net session, which clearly meant that I was not going to be a part of the side. I broke down on the way back to our team hotel.

Many cricketers struggled during that tournament as not all were able to meet their expectations. I remember one of my teammates complaining about how things could have gone better for him. He began cursing his luck but I cut him short saying, "Please let's not talk about our sad stories."

I spent too much time thinking about uncontrollable factors like team compositions, what coaches were saying and trying to work out scenarios that would help me get into the team. I kept resisting the events that were unfolding.

Looking back, had I wholeheartedly accepted the situation, I could have invested all my energy on simply working hard on the sidelines, wishing the team well and being grateful for being a part of the KPL experience. My mind would have been more cheerful and not have built up so much venom. And I would have been able to give a better account of myself when the opportunities finally came.

For I did get my chances though both were limited. In the first game I went in to bat with fewer than two overs to spare, and remained not out. Behind the wicket, I missed one stumping and effected an equally difficult one. In the second game I went into bat when we needed 54 odd runs from 16 balls. I slogged my way to a score of six, and my performance behind the stumps was average. When I got out in that second game, I returned to the pavilion and flew into a rage though fortunately none of my teammates was there to see it. We lost the game and didn't qualify for the semi-finals.

The aftermath

That night after returning to the hotel, all of us were upset. We hung around in the captain's room discussing the match. Every cricketer has his own way of handling defeat. The real professionals shrug it off as just another game, not taking the loss too personally.

Some of them would come up with reasoning that protected their confidence and image. Players were often convinced that the reasons for their failing had nothing to do with their game or skill level. Many just deflected the blame and appropriated the events that unfolded to secure their statures. Everything and anything was blamed – terrible pitches, bad luck, injuries, team management, or coaches. What actually happened and how they were eventually represented seldom matched. Memory is poetry they say.

I feel this technique worked for them because in a game like cricket where there is *no linear relationship between effort and result*, why should one even bother holding himself responsible for the outcome? (This point is elaborated in the chapter on goal-keeping). While post-match introspection is essential for learning, I think it should be more balanced with an understanding of one's own mistakes, than a merely indulgent blame game.

At the other extreme, I had a habit of always holding myself responsible for every little thing. As a result, I spent most of my prime cricketing years feeling guilty for outcomes I had no control over. Later, I found that there is an element of randomness in every sphere of life. In his book *Fooled by Randomness*, Nassim Nicholas Taleb speaks at length about how humans try to theorise random outcomes as non-random.

The 'Oh God, why me?' rant

Before all discussions concluded that night, I retired to my room at the hotel and was alone for a while. Here, away from all the chatter, I felt the full weight of my mind. I felt a deep sense of failure, anger and frustration. All this was happening in a beautiful hotel room with plasma TV, soft beds, fancy toilets and room service. I should have been enjoying all this right? But I wasn't. If one is miserable inside, it does not matter what comforts one is surrounded by outside.

In angst I decided to blame an easy target, God. "Why me, oh Lord? Why me? They say you must have passion and work hard to succeed. Please tell me if I have not done that. I will do anything it takes oh God please just tell me what I must do. You say one must have patience. I am almost 26 years old now. I have been playing this game since I was 12, how much more patience do I need? Why am I languishing in cricketing hell?"

Thus pleading I fell asleep. Some conditioning is so deep-rooted and some ego is so strong that only dramatic circumstances or occurrences trigger a change.

However bad the KPL experience was for me, I fondly recall a conversation I had with my teammate K B Pawan.[39] KB was known in cricketing circles to be a meditator. He spoke about it openly and credited all his success and turnaround – in one season he scored over 3000 runs – to his meditation. He would wake up each morning and meditate for an hour.

I noticed he never ever got flustered on the field. He had a calm Buddha-like demeanour while batting and even if he was not having the best season, he would handle it pretty well. KB is one of the nicest guys you will ever meet. He is always full of encouraging words, soft at heart yet firm and forever urging his teammates to 'stay in the present' and not worry about anything else. I wanted to know his secrets and employ them in Mumbai, where I was going to play in the Times Shield soon after.

I learnt from him what I feel is the most accurate definition of mental toughness. It is one's ability to stay focused in the present or the task on hand, regardless of the situation on the field. Ideally, this should extend off the field as well, but we sportspeople must definitely be able to do so on the field. The overriding question is, how should a mind be to make that possible?

I was not new to meditation. I had been to a Vipassana[40] camp at age 17, and left after seven days as I was unable to handle the extreme discipline. From zero hours of meditation to eight hours a day and complete silence proved to be too much of a shock to my teenage mind.

Anyway, on the team bus to Mysore that day, KB told me more about meditation and how it impacts all facets of one's life. He spoke of the importance of practicing every day, and mentioned that he heard V V S Laxman also regularly meditated. Suffice to say this conversation stirred me up. I had tried almost everything else, but this path was relatively unexplored, and here I could clearly see the impact it had on KB.

The long road back

> We can't solve problems by using the same kind of thinking we used when we created them.[41]
>
> – *Albert Einstein*

Soon after my KPL debacle, I decided the very next day that I must play at least one season of cricket with the 'ideal' frame of mind. To play 'out of happiness and not for it,' and be totally absorbed in the present. How could I rediscover the joy of playing? It was the only thing that could bring me back, and I was just not comfortable with the idea of quitting the game while I was still bitter.

First, I had to understand the factors that were preventing me from accomplishing this. I analysed threadbare my failures with the help of people close to me, who have deep insight and knowledge on various subjects. Besides Mr Kinjal Suratwala, there was Mr Rajshekar,[42] someone who painstakingly kept track of my progress not just of cricket but also that of the company I co-founded. If not for his constant support, confidence and encouragement, things would have been immeasurably more complex for me.

On analysis, I found my biggest weakness was that I cared too much about cricketing success. My entire identity and self-worth was merged with it. I feared the thought of failing. The lust for fame and attention were driving all my efforts. Many a time, when talking to my friends about my cricketing career and the multitude of frustrations I was facing, they could never understand what the fuss was all about. "Focus on your company da," they would tell me. I would view that as an insult, because I took it to mean that they did not believe I had what it took to realise my dreams. I also examined several of my character traits such as:

- I talked too much
- I was very eager to please
- I felt bad easily and took very long to recover from setbacks
- I was very easily satisfied and even more easily distracted
- I showed off when there was no real reason to
- I lacked the discipline to match my goals
- I feared and worried about everything and did not know how to unleash my cricketing potential

Collectively, these mental programs took focus away from the present and made it impossible for me to enjoy myself. I worked extremely hard and that made me feel like I owned the result.

When I failed to perform, I complained, made excuses, blamed coaches for not giving the right advice at the right time, blamed selectors for being prejudiced, blamed parents for not sending us to Bengaluru early enough. The tricky ego came up with a million reasons to exonerate and position itself to be the victim (there is a saying on a wall at the National Cricket Academy, Bengaluru – "If you should have or could have, then you would have.")

Around that time, I spoke to a close friend about my grief. He mentioned the research of the late Dr Elizabeth Kubler Ross, a Swiss-American psychiatrist. She had conducted research on death and wrote a landmark book, *On Death and Dying.* Two of her most profound conclusions are:

- Life must be accepted in its totality
- Whether you recognise it or not, "You are loved beyond comprehension."

At the time I could relate to the first point but not so much to the second. I failed to accept outcomes or take responsibility for my actions. Any healing process starts with acceptance. As long as I was blaming fate or anybody else for my failures, I was never going to address the real issues. I had to stand up and be accountable; I had the tall task of taking responsibility for all my actions. I could no longer blame others for the faults I suffered. If I was unhappy, I was the sole cause, nobody else. So the order of the day was to turn the light upon myself and not elsewhere.

I was deeply attached to the idea of becoming a cricketing star. I thought it was my ticket to a make-believe world that was devoid of misery and problems. All my training and hard work was linked to this idea. I could never truly enjoy life if I didn't have a performance to justify it. This created immense psychological pressure that was eating me from the inside out. In hindsight I tell you, it was a miserable existence and I am glad I am out of it.

I had to first forgive myself because I had been whipping myself constantly, putting myself down. Then I had to forgive and forget those who had a low opinion of me and had constantly discouraged me.

To move towards acceptance, I began aggressively writing down on a sheet of paper, "I am responsible for everything that *has happened and will happen* in my life. My actions are the causes and the effects. I am the architect of my own life. I have chosen to play cricket seriously, and will live happily with the outcome of that decision. This much is in my hands."

At last, faith in a higher power entered and I really can't say how or why exactly. It just happened. I remember writing that, "If I had to succeed, I probably would have succeeded by now. Perhaps I am not ready for what I want and out of love and grace, the Almighty is not exposing me." When I did this, I immediately felt better and lighter. Hope entered my heart once again. I showed gratitude and when I did that, the ego stepped aside. I was healed, for the time being at least. The slate was clean and I felt unburdened.

The goal was to be unperturbed and calm throughout, and succeed in all types of situations. It had become increasingly clear that I needed another type of intelligence. It was in this process of taking a serious look at my inner condition that I stumbled upon a discourse by an enlightened person.

The first insight

I had met him before but never thought much of him; my pride was too great to think he had anything to offer. One evening, an uncle of mine dragged me along for a talk in Bengaluru. I was inquisitive but quite hesitant to go, though I eventually gave in. To my surprise, unlike any previous discourses I'd been to, the speaker spoke like a friend. He didn't sound Godly or superstitious, he just sounded like a truthful human being. Known by the moniker Sri M,[43] he is a spiritual guide to many. He believes that the "Teaching is more important than the teacher."[44]

He wasted no time. The first thing he discussed was the link between knowledge, memory and the present (I will get to the explanation in the coming chapters). When he finished explaining the association, I found it to be so simple, yet so profoundly illuminating that I instantly understood what I had been doing wrong all these years. I was eager to see if I could use it to fix my thinking and become a better player.

Around the same time, my uncle gifted me a book called *The Jewel in the Lotus* authored by Sri M. It presented to me what proved to be the most crucial and invaluable insight about the world and our purpose in it. It also shed light as to the exact nature of the mind and of thought itself. In the following chapters I will focus on what I was able to grasp of those teachings.

7. Building brain into muscle – Preparation

IT'S NOT THE WILL to win that matters—everyone has that. It's the will to prepare to win that matters.

- *Paul Bryant (former American football player and coach)*

I figure practice puts your brains in your muscles.

– *Sam Snead (professional golfer)*

The more I practice, the luckier I get.

– *Gary Player (professional golfer)*

To add to all of the above, research suggests that it takes at least 10,000 hours of practice for someone to become a genius.[45] Of course practice is essential. Let me explain why so much emphasis is placed on it.

Manufactured miracles

Sachin Tendulkar's 30,000+ international runs may seem like a miracle of an achievement. But if you ask the man, I'm sure he will tell you that he put in a lot of hard work. In other fields too this holds true. While travelling by airplane, sitting on a chair in the middle of the sky is a miracle to me, it is the outcome of precise science to an aeronautical engineer.

Whether in the field of science or sport, so called miracles are a result of combining skill, talent and knowledge with hours of toil, trial, error and proper guidance. The combination then leads to insight into the laws of batting or flying a plane. In Tendulkar's case, the hours he spent at practice are well documented, and through those hours of constant practice, he became established in the fundamental laws of batting. There are laws that operate behind all 'miracles' and the person who figures out these laws becomes a miracle worker. Therefore the saying *there is a method in the madness*. Likewise for Roger Federer, Tiger Woods, Rafael Nadal and other sporting greats. *Proper, consistent execution of a scientific method or technique leads to miracles.*

At the very beginning, we all need some sort of hypothesis. For instance, when I first went to an academy, I was told to hold the bat in a certain way and stand with my legs shoulder distance apart for good balance.

The hypothesis is then put to test. If it works as desired, it becomes a theory and stays as one unless it later fails. If you want to send a rocket to the moon, you need to understand certain theoretical laws first and then proceed.

What about some players who hardly practice, and are yet so confident? Well, it's because they know they have the talent to handle the challenges on hand. They do not doubt it. Either this confidence is acquired through hours of secret practice or they are naturally gifted, and all they ever need from coaches is fine-tuning. For average players to ape them is dangerous. Instead, they must reconcile themselves to work twice as hard. And often, hardworking players overtake the really talented ones.

But ultimately confidence is a product of *knowing* that your game belongs to the very highest level and *knowing* that you have the skill to handle whatever is thrown at you. With the really talented players like Virender Sehwag or Shahid Afridi who are loaded with the 'X' factor, one never knows what's going to come next.

It seems to me they rely heavily on feeling or intuition and hence are creative, fearless and at the same time vulnerable. It's this combination that makes them exciting. They refuse to conform to a pattern. Perhaps the method in their case is to leave it to their instincts and allow their game to flow.

The other category is of those with a studious bent of mind. Though consistent, they are a bit boring at times. They do things according to a set method and stay faithful to that method in all situations. True genius is combining the right balance between unconscious intuition and conscious method and staying in that free state, albeit with that perfect combination of both aggression and caution.

Isn't concentration a result of confidence? If yes, the obvious question that follows is, what is confidence a result of? I have learnt that it's not mere preparation or hard work, but smart preparation that is needed. One of my coaches said, "The watchword is no longer practice makes perfect, it's perfect practice that makes perfect."

Essentials of preparation

> However strong the chariot may be or skilled the charioteer, till all the horses are not in unison about the path and the way through it, only hell and pandemonium rule. Nothing reigns but chaos.
>
> – *Ruzbeh Bharucha*[46]

There are several aspects to preparation on the way to achieving one's sporting goals:

- Mental
- Physical
- Technical
- Tactical
- Lifestyle

Today, thanks to various academies and fitness centres, we have a fair amount of high performance knowledge imparted on three aspects of the game – physical, technical and tactical. In my view, some critical aspects of the mental and lifestyle side are addressed insufficiently and that's what I will be addressing here.

When you apply Abraham Maslow's hierarchy of needs[47] to sport, this is what you get – physical/nutrition at the base, lifestyle/technical/tactical in the middle and mental/spiritual on top. You can add luck as a factor but that is true of anything in life.

When these factors come together in one person you get Tiger Woods, Roger Federer, Rafael Nadal, Rahul Dravid, Sachin Tendulkar and so on. Obviously one is rarely born with all the factors. One or two of these qualities could be present but the others need to be acquired and constantly worked on.

If you are technically weak, find yourself the best skills coach and iron out your flaws. If you are tactically weak, seek out and spend time with someone who is tactically brilliant. If you are physically weak, get yourself the best fitness trainer and nutritionist. If you don't like the short ball, have a million thrown at you till you figure out how to handle it. Understand the science behind it and unravel its mystery. Escaping what is not comfortable, to do only that which pleases you, is cowardice.

Always work with the best. Coaches and domain experts instil good habits and these are of the essence. You may need to work with several people as part of your preparation.

The only way to improve something you are not good at is to work at it, but in the right direction. A few years ago I cycled all the way to Nandi Hills and back, a ride of about 60 km from Bengaluru one way. I had told myself that if I could do it without stopping, I am mentally tough. But cycling to Nandi hills did nothing to make me a better player on the cricket ground. Somewhere in my mind I was equating making it to the top of the hill to success in cricket. It was foolish.

In relation to this, I want to share a short story. There was a giant ship whose engine was misfiring. Experts were summoned to fix it. They all tried and failed. Then someone suggested calling an old man who had worked his entire life in the shipyard fixing engines.

He arrived with his bag of tools and examined the engine carefully for a while. He then took out a hammer from his bag and gently tapped a certain part of the engine. The engine sprung back to life. All watching were astonished. The old man then went to the ship owner and asked for $10,000.

Shocked, the owner protested, "Why so much? You hardly did anything. You just tapped the engine. I want a proper itemised bill." The old man agreed and returned with a bill that read:

1. Tapping with hammer – $1
2. Knowing where to tap – $9,999

The moral is that intelligent effort – not blind effort – is necessary.

Intelligence and its many forms

The mental aspect of our brain can be further elaborated. It is made up of two hemispheres – the left and the right hemispheres. Though they process information differently, they are connected to and communicate with one another through the corpus callosum – the highway for information transfer.[48]

Simply put, optimal usage of our brain happens when we actively engage both hemispheres. Renowned psychologists like Howard Gardener and Daniel Goleman have spoken about various intelligences, that have been widely accepted as necessary for whole brain development.

Human intelligence and the way it is measured has changed over the years. At the beginning of the 20th century, the scientific community was mainly influenced by Aristotle's definition of man as 'a rational animal,' and this developed into a fixation with IQ (Intelligence Quotient) as the only intelligence. With IQ as the yardstick, parents, educators and doctors tested and judged a child's growth potential on the basis of IQ alone.

In 1990 Peter Salovey and John D Mayer first coined the term emotional intelligence, later made popular by Daniel Goleman. They said blending both thought/cognition with feeling/emotion is necessary to bring about optimal performance. Mr Goleman emphasises that EQ is vital for the apt use of IQ.

At the beginning of the 21st century, another 'Q' entered the fray. Arguably, this 'Q' may emerge to be the most important 'Q' of them all – 'SQ' or Spiritual Quotient.

Spiritual intelligence to me is the science behind the present moment. Everyone, not just sportspersons, must learn the art of letting go and being in the present. This organically becomes the science behind happiness as well. Being in the moment is vital to peak performance.

In this process of finding out how to be in the present, and the various conditions and habits that pulled me away from it, I was forced to ask more fundamental questions of myself. Questions like, who really am I? What is my role in this big world? Is my identity limited to what I do aka my profession, my family, my relationships?

Spiritual intelligence is not merely possessing an intellectual understanding of the answers to these questions. It lies in experiencing the answers, which *gradually unravel our true identity.*

The more I study this science, the more I begin to see that concentration, happiness, peace of mind, love, and awareness are all linked. We simply use different words in different contexts, but ultimately they are all spiritual tendencies we exhibit. If we figure out a way to build any one of these qualities, the job is done. As the French Jesuit priest Pierre Teilhard de Chardin said, "We are not physical beings having a spiritual experience; we are spiritual beings having a physical experience."[49]

Too often in India spirituality is labelled as abstract and so esoteric a science, that it is either irrelevant or meant only for a select few, or that a person has to be 'ready.' for it. Well, for what it's worth, I profoundly disagree with these notions, for spirituality is simply too crucial a science for mainstream education to ignore.

A broad classification of five widely accepted intelligences (though more have been defined) is listed below:

- Cognitive
- Emotional
- Spiritual
- Ethical
- Social

Today's education and commercial culture evolves our cognitive, logical or executive brain (the frontal lobes or prefrontal cortex) to a great degree. Detailed insight on the other two is not so commonly available.

This book mainly throws light on the other two aspects – the emotion (EQ) and intuition (SQ), or the joy inherent in the inter-circuitries of our brain's right hemisphere. Ideal performance states occur when thoughts and emotions support each other and do not work at cross-purposes.

It's rare to find a player with that perfect balance between thinking, feeling and being. I was too much of a thinker and it led me to a dead end; others relied excessively on gut feel with inconsistent results.

When emotion goes unregulated, we get overexcited and make errors. So we need logic or intellect to reign us in and bring the mind back to the task on hand. The flipside to this is that dry logic or intellect minus feeling can result in bland showings. An ideal performance state involves healthy interaction between intellect and intuition. When they combine in one person, actions will proceed from his highest nature, goodness and beauty.

Before I get to that in the following chapters, let me leave you with a short note on the importance of lifestyle.

Looking at lifestyle

To be radical in your art, you need to be conservative in your life.

– *Unknown*

Many promising careers meet dreadful ends not because of the players' skills on the field, but because of the choices they make off it. The fate of several football players, including Paul Gascoigne (who was like Tendulkar for English football in the early 1990s), makes sad reading:

> By some estimates as many as three in five former players will be declared bankrupt, often blighted by bad financial advice. At least 150 ex-professionals are currently in prison. Clarke Carlisle, chairman of the Professional Footballers' Association, believes hundreds of current players face mental health issues. More than 700 a year end up being pitched out of the sport in their 20s after failing to win a new contract.

> The former Tottenham Hotspur, Lazio and England midfielder was fined £1,000 after he admitted drunkenly assaulting a security guard at Stevenage railway station on 4 July. Gascoigne, who has battled alcoholism for many years, was fined £600 for an assault charge and £400 for a drunk and disorderly charge.

> Monday's fine was made as one of his erstwhile opponents, former Arsenal left-back Kenny Sansom, admitted to sleeping on a park bench over the weekend. It emerged that the 54-year-old, capped 86 times by England and a £1m player in 1980 when that was a huge fee, was homeless and battling alcoholism."[50]

This is not a phenomenon that is unique to a few countries alone. India has its fair share of prodigies who have succumbed to poor choices off the field.

I know of a former junior India player who would smoke a cigarette till the last minute, and put it out just before he went into bat. And he would smash the bowlers all over the place without breaking a sweat. He also bowled brilliantly – on his day he was unplayable. He could have been the all-rounder India was looking for. But he refused to get his hand off the self-destruct button. Besides smoking, he drank himself silly and withered away. What a waste!

I always wished I could bat like him or at least share the same confidence. He had God-given talent and method, but lacked balance off the field.

Social and moral intelligence

> The world is a moral gymnasium wherein we all have to exercise to become stronger and stronger spiritually.
>
> – *Swami Vivekananda*[51]

Spiritual and moral growth goes hand in hand. One cannot exist without the other. I know morality is a complex issue with diverse definitions and viewpoints. The argument of what is right and wrong and can go on forever. However, what spiritual intelligence does is to gradually provide a better understanding of 'who we really are' i.e., the bigger picture. And with that understanding comes greater clarity.

Once our priorities are in place, there is clarity in thinking and this directly impacts decision making in society. Therefore, when IQ, EQ and SQ combine, it leads to the maturing of both moral and social intelligence.

Here in India we are greatly supported by a strong family structure that cares for us, shares our burdens and enforces certain values that protect us. But the family system is increasingly coming under threat. Recently, I heard an uncle caustically remark, "If you want to make good human beings out of cricketers, please send them to ashrams, not to sports academies." He said this in response to a former India player who suggested that being a good human being was as important, if not more, than being a good cricketer.

We need to guard against moral cynicism. If we really want to, ethics can be taught in a very interesting manner and made lively. For example, coaches can have sessions where they come up with mock situations and ask a player how he would react, both on and off the field. Many players get into trouble because they are unaware of the moral traps that others can lay.

In the coming chapters I will paraphrase and quote teachings from the book *Jewel in the Lotus,* and my interactions with its author. I describe the way I made my life a great deal more fulfilling by overcoming long residing mental blocks.

8. Thinking about thinking

WHEN DISMISSED by a bowler early in my innings, sledged at during a match, rejected by selectors, or dumped by my beautiful girlfriend, what really causes me to hurt? Does the suffering lie in the incident or in my thinking, which then gets stored away in my memory? Life is shaped on the basis of thoughts that we choose to associate with or hang onto. While growing up, we are all groomed to think a certain way and that determines our response to challenge.

Regardless of our backgrounds, we experience life through our thoughts, and the corresponding emotions that come with it. I guess that's fairly obvious. That being the case, let's take a closer look at the very nature of thought from a different standpoint. We'll use the ancient Indian technique of understanding the external world by analysing what's happening inside our minds.

Thoughts at play

Why is the word 'play' used? The anecdote below illustrates this.

A wooden stump about the height of a human being stands at the centre of a thickly wooded park. Visibility around the area of the stump is quite poor. A thief comes across it and thinking that it might be a police officer, runs for safety. A lover, thinking it might be her beloved, feels passion. A young boy, thinking it might be his mother, runs to it for comfort. But all along, the stump remained what it originally was, a stump. It was just the mind that was at play. We only see what we're conditioned to see. There is a saying that, 'If God were to appear before a pickpocket, all the pickpocket would see are His pockets.'

When we evaluate, assess, compare, measure, scrutinise and decide, what we're really doing is thinking. And thinking is a continuous, habitual and reflexive process. Our feelings of hurt or good memories are ultimately manifested to us in the form of thought.

Our brain supplies information that forms these thoughts. What sends information to our brain? Our senses. What is their credibility in providing accurate information? This question is important because senses influence how we look at the world.

I've listed below the nature of information received from the senses:

- Imperfect
- Temporary
- Relative

I'll describe each of these in a little more detail.

Imperfect

You are standing on a beach at dusk observing the setting sun, beautiful as it is. What do you notice? You see that as time passes the sun gradually descends and disappears out of sight, as if into the water. On observing this, you think the sun has moved to the other side of the globe right?

But science tells us that the sun doesn't rise or set. It is the earth that spins. It only follows that what the eyes see and the mind perceives, is in this case completely divorced from fact. In fact, the other senses – ears/sound, nose/smell, taste/tongue and touch – are not always perfect and cannot always be trusted.

Yet, based on sensory information, the brain determines the course of action i.e., what to say or think, or how to act. As such the values, beliefs, and ideas that often arise in our minds could be faulty. This could be the cause of all the mental blocks, prejudices and acrobatics that follow. We rarely know what fact is and what we treat as fact is only relative to our understanding – a framework within whose confines we operate.

Knowledge made available through technology such as video analysis is not always faultless. A player can always upgrade his skills. If the video you're analysing of him does not contain the upgrade he has made, your understanding will be imperfect and the tactics that follow will be incorrect.

Surely the insights made available through technology must be used, but conclusions drawn can never be treated as perfect. Moreover, human nature is unpredictable. Attempts to make it predictable by using scientific tools succeed only in creating an 'illusion of control' that quite often becomes unstuck.

That said, it's important to note that physical fear is not unreal. The fears of being run over by a truck, falling off a building or getting hit on the body are very real.[52] That's why man wisely invented protective equipment to shield himself; the irony is that he seems a lot less concerned about similar protection against the daily assaults on his mind.

Long story short, my senses are incapable of giving me the full picture. Almost always they provide perspectives and thoughts that are only partially accurate or half-truths. It only follows that thoughts arising from such knowledge are of the very same nature.

Temporary

I remember thinking that I would never recover from three big moments of pain in my life:

1. The pain of a dropped catch that cost my team a match
2. The breakup with my first girlfriend
3. The pain of rejection at not being initially picked for the state Under-16 team.

I'll briefly describe each of these incidents below.

1. I once dropped a catch at a crucial stage of a quarter final match and this helped the opponents win the game. I felt so guilty and ashamed for what I had done, that I was too embarrassed to even show my face to my teammates. I escaped the situation by switching clubs. But two years later, I re-joined that club and played for more four years during which time I even captained. Not once was the dropped-catch mentioned.
2. My first breakup was the most painful and depressing experience of my life. The day after she broke up with me, I had a match and batted with tears in my eyes. For close to a year, I would wake up every morning feeling miserable and desperate. It was a living hell. I felt that unless my ex-girlfriend was to somehow become a part of my life again, I could never be happy. That was the extent of my sensory driven delusion. I could not bear the shame of being dumped. I conjured up visuals of the girl being with some other boy, and believed that I wasn't good enough. This feeling lasted for so long that I was convinced the pain would never abate.
3. After scoring an unbeaten 132 in the finals of an Under-16 KSCA state selection match, I was shocked at not being named in the final squad. More so because the cricketing grapevine indicated that I was a certainty. I thought my world had come to an end.

> The pain of rejection was very real. After a couple of matches, I made it into the squad and was as intensely happy as I was previously sad.

If you look closely at these incidents, you will find a common thread linking them. *The illusion of permanency* is what made them so hard to deal with.

Now the questions that come to my mind are:

- Were all the upheavals based on fact?
- Were any of them going to last forever as I was making it out to be?
- Is it wrong for me to call them illusions?

Of course, the answer I got was an overwhelming no! Memory fades and as time passes, none of what was important back then is of any value today. This is the true nature of all pleasure and pain. Whatever one is going through will disappear and die, because that is its very nature. The minute one becomes aware of this, things begin to change. If my mind had been better trained in these matters, I would not be so under or over-emphatic with regard to the above events.

There are so many matches one plays that a good catch erases the memory of a dropped one and vice-versa. Every player who is worth his salt will tell you that failure is as much an illusion as success; one does not exist without the other, and in fact *nothing fails like success*.

The difference between the professional mind and that of the amateur's is that the former does not give his success or failure more importance than necessary. The professional understands the two-faced, alternating and unpredictable relationship between effort and result, and accepts it wholeheartedly.

Ultimately, as hard as the above-related experiences were to endure, they eventually did teach me to better understand the fickle nature of thought and the world of the senses. In the sensual plane, change is the only reality. We find that good form gives way to bad form, success to failure, joy to sorrow and so on. This duality persists universally and all of mankind is subject to it.

A common saying in sporting parlance is, 'Form is temporary. Class is permanent.' Now if the word class and its permanency were to be seen through a spiritual lens, perhaps it would take on a whole new meaning.

Relative

What does 'relative' mean, you may wonder. Take a closer look and you'll see that the relative nature of the senses pervades everything.

One summer several years ago, I was feeling sad after a string of low scores. My karate/yoga sir, Mr Dhruve, asked me, "What is it that you want from life?" The pain I was feeling prompted me to say, "I guess right now I just want to be happy." He replied, "I know someone who works at a cancer hospital. I will take you there and once you see the suffering, you will realise how lucky you are, and how petty your problems are in comparison."

Simply by relating to the perspective shown, I calmed down. For a moment, my mind saw the larger picture and moved beyond its own concerns. My so-called worries disappeared when I understood how insignificant they were in relation to the suffering of millions of others. And instead of whining about my failure to score runs or fretting about competition, I felt foolish and thanked God for all that He had blessed me with. And when I showed gratitude, I always felt better.

All that aside, the real reason we say our wants and experiences are relative in nature is that they can be compared or rated. My perception of a bowler or opponent's skill levels are sometimes different from the way my teammate perceives them. Each has his own view based on his knowledge, confidence and understanding of the opponent. A good example is how several international batsmen find Lasith Malinga difficult to handle, but Virat Kohli appears to play him with relative ease.

Similarly, we can compare Sachin Tendulkar's career to that of Don Bradman's. In deciding who the better player is, some will say Sachin and some will say Bradman, and the conclusions can be debated endlessly, without ever arriving at a definite answer.

As the saying goes, "One man's food is another man's poison." Palates and cuisines differ in various lands. What is staple diet in some parts of China will be considered inedible in India. Likewise, sporting tastes also vary. Cricket, a religion in India, is unheard of in many parts of the world.

You'll always find someone more successful, more talented, better looking, wealthier, more important or more evolved. In the same breath you will find millions who are born with physical, financial or emotional challenges, struggling to survive. How we respond to all this depends on our relative view of the world.

Speaking of relativity, Einstein said it best: "Put your hand on a hot stove for two seconds and it seems like two hours. Sit with a beautiful girl for two hours and it seems like two minutes."

When it comes to selections, many a time our perception of our own skill levels and performance differs with that of the selectors. I thought I deserved a place in that Under-16 state team, but the selectors thought differently. Again, there can strictly be no *right or wrong*, they had their rationale and I had mine.

So really, how real are thoughts?

I struggle to recall details of memories over a decade old. Were the memories 'real' in the strict sense of the term, they would continue to haunt and hurt me. But the fact is that a hundred erases the memory of a duck and vice versa. A thought that brought me happiness yesterday causes me grief today and an idea that made me popular yesterday has lost its relevance today.

How then can thought, something that is so fickle, there one moment and gone the next, ever be considered real? Every construct of the mind is merely a temporary truth and will someday cease to be relevant or die with me. Only that which is real in the true sense is always relevant. Strictly speaking, that which holds true only for a short time and kept alive temporarily by thought, is unreal.

Mental blocks

All mental blocks are a result of wrong knowledge. Our true nature is happiness or energy which is 'block-free.' So if you aren't happy or energetic, it simply means some delusion is blocking that happiness or energy from bursting forth.

Blocks cannot survive too long when the mind comes upon knowledge or insight. I experienced intense mental blocks for years *only because my thinking rested on certain beliefs that gave those occurrences a lot more importance than they deserved*.

Once I understood 'failure' to be an inevitable part of the game, that even the best of players goof up, I lost all guilt. What mattered was putting in my best effort and if that was there, there was no room for guilt.

How thoughts create personality

Associating with thoughts not only creates but reinforces personality or ego. For instance, once the mind thinks of itself as a cricketer, all its ambitions and actions move in the direction of building for itself a flourishing cricketing career. It views anything that comes in the way of realising that ambition as a threat. This perception leads to hostile feelings towards so-called 'competitors' and eventually attracts stress.

By force of habit I instinctively identify with my thoughts and treat them as real and because of this habit, I sometimes suffer and sometimes rejoice. So long as my mind thinks and receives only good and positive images, I am happy. Sadly, I find that I am often afflicted and consumed by negative thoughts, and hence fear is bound to enter my mind.

My first task is to disengage from all deflating thought patterns, by slowly seeing through relative, imperfect and temporary truths. All conflict arises from treating temporary and relative truths as permanent and absolute.

Now having studied and gathered knowledge on the true nature of thought, let's understand its place in the overall scheme of things.

Putting knowledge in its place

Growing up, most of us are taught that knowledge is power. If I do not have knowledge of the letters of the alphabet, how can I read or write? If I do not have knowledge of how to drive a car, how do I drive? If I do not have knowledge that comes with an MBA, how to do I manage a big corporation and earn a livelihood? Knowledge comes from theory and experience. It leads to skill that pays and is greatly revered. Yes, knowledge is power, and this holds true for most professions in the world.

But knowledge is not enough. Along with technical and tactical knowledge, what is required is awareness of the present moment. I have seen many top players detest too much thinking, simply because they find that it clutters and burdens the mind, and causes them to get lost in thought. I have found that *thinking too much* curtails your natural flair. On the contrary when you don't think at all, you become like an animal. So here's something from Sri M's book *The Jewel in the Lotus* that puts knowledge in its proper place:

> Let us say that you have walked into a field full of thistles and you have thorns lodged in your feet. You did not know – you were ignorant – that it was a thorny terrain. You try to pull them out with your bare hands, but to no avail; they are in too deep for that.

> So, you find a sharper, longer and sturdier thorn to remove them. Similarly, you remove the thorns of ignorance and pain with the thorn of knowledge. Tell me, will you, after getting rid of the painful thorns, stick the larger thorn into your feet? No, you won't; you will throw it away. So it is with the thorn of knowledge we remove the thorn of ignorance and both of them are discarded for freedom from the thorns.[53]

The role of the second thorn – knowledge – is to remove ignorance. It is used simply as a tool. Once the job is done, it is discarded, just as one would walk away from a boat after it has been used for crossing a river. Similarly technique is also knowledge, but to make the best use of it, one must be free and not bound by it.

THE RIGHT KNOWLEDGE

Right knowledge is that which helps us tune our senses and rational faculties to be able to differentiate the permanent from the temporary, the relative from the real and the perfect from the flawed. Decision-making based on these parameters can then be said to be of a spiritual nature. Here again, I would like to share a passage from Sri M's book:

> Before we go any further, let us see what knowledge itself is. You understand a thing or an event and say, "I've acquired knowledge of that." This means that you have stored all the information or as much as you can get regarding that thing or event in your memory, so that you can refer back to it, recognise and react to it, in the future. All knowledge is like that –that which is stored in one's memory. Can you think of any other? The moment you have listened to my words they have vanished from the present and have become things of the past. They now constitute memory, and memory is a thing of the past. Knowledge, as we know it is then something that you remember, whether it is from the recent past, a split second ago, or years ago. That is, it is memory. All knowledge is, therefore, memory – a thing of the past.[54]

And the present is 'here and now,' ever fresh, new, original and untouched by memory or the past. We can gather that in the quest for the perfect 'present,' we are doing ourselves a big disservice if we *only rely* on technique or expertise or any other form of knowledge, as they too are memories. We must simply let go of it all.

Water in a flowing river is never the same at any point. Likewise, every moment can be treated as a new beginning; this is not just a philosophical point but a scientifically accurate assertion. As I write this, cells in my body are dying and brand new ones are being born every moment.

Our conditioned minds are storehouses of canvases filled with a collection of paintings from past experiences. Each canvas corresponds to an event and produces a memory *out of which thoughts and actions arise*. In contrast, the present in its original state is similar to a fresh canvas; blank and open to all possibilities and outcomes.

The mind clings to memory; it is in the habit of comparing and referencing the 'now.' For example, 'This bowler got me out the last time I played him' – the mind uses the experience of 'what was' and draws up 'what will be.' A mind with such a pattern becomes a machine, operating only from memory or background. The present is looked at either through the screen of the past or dreams of the future. The experience of the 'here and now' is diluted.

As each moment passes, more past is added, and the more the mind becomes conditioned. But the present is the only 'real' thing that exists. The past and future are both fiction.

To see the present as it is, the mind must break the patterns it is subject to. Instead of hoarding all the canvases in our mind, we must let go of them or carry our achievements and disappointments lightly.

Let's get practical

All this philosophy is no joke; it is meant to be realised. Phrases such as, 'be in the present,' 'focus on the task,' and 'one-pointedness,' are all different words talking about a very high quality of attention or awareness. Most of you have probably already experienced this when you've been completely engrossed in a game, a song or anything that absorbs you.

In the case of batting for long periods, a challenging task that requires one to stay mentally fresh, sometimes the very thought of batting six hours on a hot day can get one down. The times when I succeeded, I often thought in this manner:

- Every ball is new and has never been bowled before, so let me enjoy it
- This is the first time this ball is ever being bowled

This kind of thinking kept me mentally fresh, involved, excited and eager over long durations. Otherwise, with over six hours of batting, one's mind can very easily become stale and the whole process of batting can seem repetitive. When one is in the moment, one hardly ever tires; instead the process becomes fun. One is free of the incidents of the past delivery, and the next ball beckons filled with possibilities.

In cricket it is 'one ball at a time,' for golf it is 'one shot at a time,' for tennis, table tennis and badminton it is 'one point at a time,' and so on.

Being free, fearless and accepting

To be free is to be happy. The ultimate purpose behind all struggles and goals is happiness. The aspirations and goals that drive us, and the personalities we adopt and groom over time to achieve these goals have only one purpose: to find happiness. If we have it we don't need anything else.

Happiness that results from indulging senses cannot really be called happiness. Temporary feelings are sensations, like what you feel when you buy a new gadget. The sensation is linked to the gadget and when the newness of it disappears, so will the sensation. When one has an ice bath you know the icy cool feeling will soon subside because you don't become the ice. When senses are involved it's more about temporary pleasures that come and go between sorrows. They are a crude form of happiness.

What we are always seeking is permanency. We don't want things to change. We do not want the quality of joy to diminish with time. We seek happiness that is untouched by incident, circumstance or condition, happiness that continues forever.

We jump jobs, matches or relationships, hoping that something might happen that will permanently drive out sorrow. But when we examine our life, we see that this rarely happens.

When we look for happiness outside ourselves, we try to control uncontrollables (result or outcome) to bring about that feeling. In psychological terms, to use reward as motivation is called extrinsic motivation. In such a pursuit, the nature of the happiness that results will always be fleeting. Where then is the permanency I seek? As Sri M says:

> I seek joy, and sorrow raises its ugly head. I get hold of what I desire and then comes the fear of losing it, of somebody taking it away, or losing it when I die. I see the beautiful moon, and time the great

> snatcher, snatches it away and I am left with an image I keep craving for again.
>
> You experience joy when coming into contact with the objects of the world. But the joy wells up in your own heart, doesn't it? When you see the Taj Mahal, does the enjoyment take place in the monument or in your heart? All joys spring forth from within your being, my dear friend. The reservoir of all joy, the essence of all bliss, is in your heart, in the core of your own being.[55]

We all have the potential for joy inside us right now. Not in the future or the past. I say potential because some of our mental and emotional programs are such that all the joy in our hearts is caged by certain self-imposed conditions. If one can tap into that feeling of happiness at will and work out of that happiness, then the action that follows is of one's highest nature. This is a very practical suggestion as happiness resides in the present moment.

All my life, my mind was so conditioned that peace was never in my hands, and worse still, I was not even conscious of it. I kept the company of sophisticated viewpoints and theories that ensured it stayed that way.

Understanding all this had a profound impact. I saw that my happiness or self-worth was in fact independent of everything, including my performance. I thought, "Oh my God, what a donkey I am." It was an epiphany of sorts that changed my life.

9. That indefinable something

HAVING DEALT WITH the basic anatomy of thought in the previous chapter, the questions that come to mind are, is there anything at all that is not subject to this fickle, temporary and ever changing nature? What does the present moment feel like or look like? Can it be described? If our thoughts and personality are not real, what do we have to look forward to? In this chapter, let's explore these questions further with an open mind before arriving at any conclusion.

We are intuitive

> The intuitive mind is a sacred gift and the rational mind a faithful servant. We have created a society that honours the servant and has forgotten the gift.
>
> – *Albert Einstein*

Is there a way for us to tap into the intuitive mind on a more regular basis or is it something we have no control over? Sri M cites the *conditioned mind* as the obstacle. The anecdote below explains the power of this gift in a way that simplified it for me.

> A wise old man with rags was literally dragging himself along the side of a busy road in a big city. He was so weak that every step he took seemed to be a painful ordeal. All of a sudden a car coming at full speed screeched to a halt, its horn blaring just behind him. Now, almost a miracle took place. The old man who, seconds ago looked as if he would fall and die any moment, leapt on to the footpath and at a safe distance from the car.
>
> How did he do that? A moment earlier, he couldn't have had any inkling of the imminent danger, so that he could save himself. Then what saved him? It was a split second reflex action. The message 'jump and save your life' must have flashed into his brain from the

> supreme director (or intuitive mind), and the message was transmitted instantly to his limbs. Adrenalin was released immediately and the muscles reacted.
>
> The point to note here is that there was no interference from the conditioned mind and the prejudiced thought processes. If thought had interfered, he couldn't have jumped away from the wheels. He would instead still be having thoughts like, "How can a man weak like me jump out of the car's way when I don't even have the energy to walk?" while the vehicle crushed him under its wheels. In this emergency situation, the message 'jump' came directly without being conditioned and influenced by thought.[56]

Without exception, all of us at some point will have done something brilliant and later pondered, 'How did I manage that?' In my case, every time I have done something special with the bat or gloves, I subsequently realised that at those times, thoughts were scarce. I had batted almost as if on auto mode; not thinking about anything in particular. At other times, I managed to perform similarly by forcefully subduing my ego. But the ego seldom recedes and consistent intuitive action eludes us.

Is there a fourth state?

Let's try forming a basic rational idea of the source of intuitive intelligence. Does it proceed from within us or from our neighbour's house or some place far away in the mountains, or does it come from the sky?

In the course of our lives, we regularly experience three states of consciousness: the waking, dream and deep sleep states. Let's look into the first two states – the waking and dream states.

As you read these words, you are doing so in the 'waking state' and when you sleep and have a dream, you are in the 'dream state,' that's fairly obvious. When we are awake, our dream state is unreal and vice-versa. However, we are *aware* in both these states, because we *know* what has transpired both when we're awake and in our dream.

Several times in my dream I've experienced falling from a tall building and no other reality exists except the fear of falling and dying. Just as I am about to hit the ground and shatter my bones, I wake up panting and sweating, relieved that it was just a dream. But in the dream it feels absolutely real.

This goes to show that at some level my brain is active. It reacts to the fear, causing my body's physiological process to kick in. In this aspect the dream state is as real or unreal as the waking state, as there's a consciousness or awareness that operates in both.

But in deep sleep there is no awareness of any other state of consciousness. There is no ego or I. The 'I' that we hold so dear in the waking state disappears in deep sleep that takes with it all our problems and worries. We are for all purposes dead to the world. You enjoy a peace and bliss without being impacted by the internal world of dreams and the external world of the senses; deep sleep is a *content-less experience*. On analysing it you really can't say if you were conscious or unconscious, you may even question whether there is any consciousness.

This is what makes deep sleep so endearing to humanity. It is nature's gift to man, where we completely let go and forget all the baggage connected to being someone; we wake up feeling completely refreshed. Deep sleep is also proof that the ego is so unreal and illusionary, it cannot even survive sleep.

But how can there be no consciousness, if on waking up you say, 'I had a wonderful, undisturbed sleep?' Undoubtedly, there is *something* during deep sleep that is capable of experiencing that state of tranquillity.[57]

That something is inside us. It knows that you slept like a log without a thought, a dream or a nightmare. The masters of the east describe this state as the fourth state of consciousness or *Turiya*. In attempting to describe this state they have said, "It moves yet it moves not,"[58] and "It is far yet it is near." Western philosophers have said, "It has its centre everywhere and circumference nowhere," meaning it is infinite, expansive, everywhere, within and without.

All these explanations are oxymoronic and this is where spiritual realities stop appealing to the strictly scientific minded. They may question, "How can something be both far and near? It just does not make sense."

Simply put there is something more than our ordinary linear thinking, where all problems related to ego, ambitions, relationships and so on don't matter. The direct experience of it (not in sleep or just an intellectual understanding) is what is termed as realisation of the self. This is the true self from where all intelligence and intuition informs us.

Examining our reality

Could this presence or awareness, which is present in all the three states of consciousness, yet independent of it, be our true identity? Will the direct perception of it render the 'waking state' a mere dream?

Just imagine looking at the waking state the same way we currently treat our 'dream state.' If this hypothesis is in fact true (as all spiritual masters claim), just think of a person who has realised the 'fourth state.' What an impact the realisation would have on his waking state psychology. Imagine what it would be like to wake up to a state more real than the one we take to be real!

Like a multiplex movie screen there perhaps exists in us an unseen, eternally still screen on which the movie of life plays, watched by a witness without whom the movie could not be enjoyed to the fullest. While watching this movie you've probably cried, laughed, fought, forgiven, loved and lost. This could be no different from the way you would feel while watching a good movie, where you completely identified with the characters and were immersed in the experience.

It could well be that the waking state that we refer to and think of as 'reality' is not what we think it is. But to know that, we must first wake up to it isn't it?

Getting to the core

The centre of a storm is called the 'eye.' The eye is absolutely still and it is this stillness that causes all the fury. It seems as though *stillness is a necessary condition for movement*.

'That' say the seers, is reflected when the mind is utterly still and free from the influence of thoughts. This stillness is nothing but meditation. An utterly still mind performs perfect action. The comparison is made to a lake that is calm, without a ripple on its surface, for only then can you clearly see what lies below the surface. The goal of all meditation therefore is to still the mind, so that we can see that core and realise our true nature – a reservoir of unending bliss, joy, and happiness, that puts an end to all ruin.

The roots of a tree are normally unseen, but the tree and its branches exist because of the roots. Likewise, human beings could be similarly rooted in something that is hidden from our normal view. The highly individualistic nature of society roots us in personality or ego and its ideas, making it hard for alternative thoughts to come about.

Perhaps all experiences in life are meant to uncover these roots, little by little, to reveal the source present at the core of our being. The quest for that core is the spiritual journey.

THOUGHT VS THOUGHT

The whole battle of life is fought on the field of the mind. Earlier I spoke of how direct messages from our intuitive brain are constantly flowing, but we don't consistently receive them. This is because they are thwarted by the programmed mind that separates us from our centre. When you look at it that way, the mind and its thoughts become *obstacles*.

Yet it is the very same mind when coaxed and constantly reminded of its own nature, calms down and recovers its ability to receive intuitive information. When this happens the mind becomes a *path* to a greater journey.

The method of coaxing the mind often involves self-talk. Even meditation is an activity in which the mind watches itself. In a way, inside our heads at any given time there could be two or more minds at war. Thought struggles against thought, not knowing they are of the very same nature.

One part of your mind considers someone as good, automatically making someone else bad. Then the good thought strives to set the bad straight. Now, what the mind calls good and what it calls bad are both thoughts. The fact is there are no two minds, there is only one. The separation is an artificial one, raised by thought itself.

It is this divergence of minds that leads to all the conflict. In daily life the mind essays various roles – sometimes it makes me a villain and sometimes a hero. It can be the path or obstacle, a friend or enemy, and these opposite states are quite often simply a thought away.

One of the many benefits of meditation is it helps us see all these thought separations as false. In deep concentration or meditation all such artificially erected separations are removed, making the mind united. It is free from the pounding it suffers by its own constant rise and fall. The very idea that there is something in us that remains unaltered while everything changes was exciting enough to make me inquisitive about it.

The journey towards any kind of transformation that is sustainable and reliable usually requires time and consistent effort. So I made up my mind to sit down every day and put all that I'd learnt to test. I was able to put to good use the privacy offered by the room I was given at the DY Patil Club in Mumbai.

10. Home-made happiness

FROM MY previous Vipassana experience, I assigned myself the task of meditating by observing my breath. I also followed a suggestion to visualise a beautiful object or scenery before starting to focus attention on my breath. Gradually, I noticed things changing.

As I closed my eyes each day, I was first confronted with a continuous stream of images and thoughts. I struggled to ignore them. I got caught up, and still do. Each thought had a story to tell and being accustomed to indulging them, I got helplessly sucked in. When my mind was concentrated on the breath, it seemed relatively calm, but the sheer force of my past impressions kept pulling the focus away from it. Sometimes it took a while before I realised I had strayed.

The big breakthrough came when I discovered that my mind was willing to rule against itself. I cornered my mind with overwhelming evidence and told it, "I have given you too much importance all these years, woven idea over idea, theory over theory and pattern over pattern, all of which have ended in pain."

For no matter how convincing or brilliant a perspective, as long as it is meant to further my ego or please another, it is born out of anxious thought and eventually agitates the mind. I also learnt that the ego is very tricky; it felt threatened by this novel direction I was pursuing. It resented the change. It wanted to continue with its old ways, as it felt that was the only way it would remain relevant.

Soon I understood that when I successfully disengaged from thoughts, I also disengaged from personality. In doing so I delivered a blow to the ego, which wouldn't take it lying down. It fought back against the 'spiritual thought.' I began to think of my battles with the ego as a boxing match, comprised of several rounds.

Round one: Me vs me

In this round, my mind threw up all my skeletons and showed me the faces of all those I abhor. It replayed and reminded me of all incidents and humiliations I suffered on and off the field. It told me, "Like every other time, this time too you will fail. Don't you get it man you are a loser, quit trying and give in!"

It sometimes became too much to bear. What I wanted was freedom from the gnawing feeling that often told me I wasn't good enough. Earlier, every time I felt this way I would do something pleasurable to make the pain go away, postponing the problem and then justifying it.

But this time I began to comprehend it better and understood the following:

- The patterns it operated in
- The types of thoughts that were destroying my focus and also the values fuelling them

Round 2: My counter

Although I was fighting my mind, I saw that it was imperative to nurse it with care. I had to make everything seem very simple and doable. I prepared a checklist to remind myself of the following:[59]

- All I need to do is focus on one breath each time. Now is this not doable buddy?
- The only thing that exists in this world is the present breath. So keep your mind firmly fixed on it. It is the only thing that is real.[60]
- No matter what thought or image the tricky mind throws at me, I should not get aggressive. I should simply smile at it as if to say, 'Please come do what you want. I am no longer afraid, because in the end you are just a thought.'
- The thought's survival depends on me and not the other way around. Thoughts are powerless when I give them no importance.
- I should be wary of flattering thoughts as well because though they make me happy, the result can be dangerous as *they too take me away from the present.*

The idea was to practice dispassion by treating all thoughts the same. No special treatment was to be given to any one particular thought, even if they were thoughts like:

- Playing for India
- Fearing not scoring runs
- Having sex
- Fearing being dropped from the side

- Scoring a hundred and becoming a hero
- Seeing the face of someone I hate

Around the time I began my meditation practice, there was a very beautiful girl showering me with a great deal of affection. She was saying things I always wanted to hear from my dream girl. But since I was serious about executing this 'thoughts are not real' hypothesis, with great difficulty I managed to resist her charms. She eventually got fed up and started to hate my guts. That hurt! Cut up, I soon realised that it was only momentary.

The manipulative mind said, "Wah, Ashwath you are a great guy, you have fought it out and you have prevailed." I noticed this kind of thinking that pleased the ego was more dangerous than negativity, because it slyly pulled me away from focusing.

I had also read that vegetarian food was conducive to concentration. So 90% of my food intake became vegetarian. I still continue with that because I feel a lot more healthy and energetic.

As time passed, here is how I began to perceive a negative thought. Say you are walking up some stairs. You're not aware that a friend of yours is in the mood for a prank. He has hidden behind a wall waiting to scare you. As you approach the top, he jumps out of hiding and screams. In that moment, your heart skips a beat and you are terribly frightened. However, you almost instantly calm down when you see that it was only your friend playing a prank.

Similarly, negative thoughts are like those friends who are constantly playing pranks. All negative thoughts are 'pranksters' simply because our true nature is happiness and not depression. No one in this world sets out to seek depression.

In summary, three things are very clear:

- A good thought makes me feel good and a bad thought pulls me down. *Both take me away from the present or my breath*, and so in that sense, both are distracting.
- I see how thoughts die out after a certain time; I experience the truth of *thought being unreal*.
- Thoughts ought not to be worshipped. They are as much a part of the problem as they are of the solution.

Armed now with this experiential understanding, I watched my thoughts without attaching the same importance to them I once did. Because of that I was able to let them go easily. Slowly, thoughts began passing through my mind without leaving a mark, *just as a bird flies through the sky without leaving a trace or just as water bounces off the surface of a rock.* Introspecting every day, I have become calmer and more familiar with my inner condition.

When you have a physical injury, say an ankle or a groin injury, it is relatively simple to locate and treat. An X-ray will find the problem and a doctor will fix it. When it comes to our minds we cannot hold an injurious thought in our hands, take a spanner and physically remove it. The process is entirely mental, and only *you* can truly know and treat *your* condition.

This can generate an altogether different impulse that keeps the mind free, fearless and focused in the present. Try it out for yourself!

Round 3: After the clouds comes sunshine

Practicing regularly, twice a day for an hour each time for over three months, I began to notice changes. I was responding better to conditions that normally overwhelmed me in a negative way. I either let them pass or simply countered them with other thoughts.[61]

I also noted the results of this method in the Times Shield, in which I played crucial knocks under pressure and averaged close to 60. It was the best I had done in years, especially considering that I batted the last four of those innings with a dislocated little finger and a bruised ankle.

I gradually became aware of a blissful feeling of contentment. Perhaps free from the influence of gnawing thoughts, I was experiencing the joy that was always in me. In that state, there is complete acceptance and love. I felt good, positive and energetic about everything. *By looking within myself, I became more confident of the theory I spoke about in the previous chapters.* But I must add here that becoming irreversibly established in this state is a whole different ball game.

A home-made recipe

The fact that joy exists in us is quite an obvious thing. It's not speculative philosophy. Let me explain this with a Mullah Nasruddin story. But first, a little about Mullah Nasruddin. He was a wise man who lived centuries ago in Central Asia, and his stories are often used to explain simple spiritual truths. This particular story goes like this.

One day Mullah Nasruddin publicly announced that he was a smuggler. This enraged the customs officials who guarded the border areas. Every time Mullah Nasruddin arrived with his donkeys loaded with goods, both he and his cargo were thoroughly examined. The officials sometimes even burnt the grass he carried, to find out how he concealed the illegal goods. Despite all their efforts the officials found nothing.

After several years, one of the customs officials at the border retired. He had by then become Mullah Nasruddin's friend and asked him, "I don't work anymore, can you please tell me what you were smuggling?"

"Donkeys," replied Mullah Nasruddin nonchalantly.

The customs officials missed what was 'hiding' in plain sight. Similarly, if only we could look closer at ourselves, perhaps then we would know that *this joy is nearer to us than we think*.

Though I understand all this in a small way, thoughts continue to flow. When I identify with my thoughts, that 'bliss' is not experienced. And I know that to stabilise the feeling, I need to practice regularly. It is a feeling that is of the very same nature, if not better, as the one I experienced when I score a century or complete a great catch.

The only difference here is that the happiness is triggered independently, by myself and in that sense *it is home made*. It has nothing to do with scoring a hundred or receiving somebody's approval. The notion I previously held, of performance in cricket being the only thing capable of making me feel fulfilled, was dealt a body blow.

Every time I step out onto the field with this 'home-made bliss,' I play from a peaceful state of mind. This peace is no longer linked to result. I play out of love, with no feelings of jealousy or competition. It relaxes me and allows me to smile more, taking away all the pressures and fears; this immediately gives me an edge.

I play for fun and with innocence, just like I used to as a child. I am fearless about outcome and am able to focus better. All this makes me not only a better performer, but also a better teammate and human being.

THE BIG QUESTION

When I ask myself, *"Who really am I?"* I get a different answer to the one I got when my identity was muddled up with wealth, status and ego. My mind wonders, "Maybe the joy I experience when not caught up with Ashwath's conditioned thoughts is my real nature, not Ashwath the cricketer who has to play for India or die."

To experience that feeling of joy day in and day out, independent of external circumstances and free of any strings, *some comfort zones had to be sacrificed*. The knowledge and values around which the new me had to be realigned were now available, thanks to my new friend and guide, Sri M.

I would like to again emphasise that what really struck me was understanding that the potential for complete happiness and fulfilment lay within my own heart. That I didn't have to seek it elsewhere. And when I looked at life from that standpoint, automatically the mind stopped stressing. I knew everything would be *ok* even if I 'failed' to achieve my cricketing ambitions or anything else I'd set out to do in the future.

Ultimately, the goal is not to become unconscious. Of course we need our mind for everything we do. But perhaps, by understanding its true nature, there's a possibility of increasing happiness in our lives.

You may ask, "But how to become detached or disengaged with thoughts?" Practice it. If you have been practicing attachment for 20 years, it will probably take you a while to cultivate detachment. Can you reverse a habit formed over 20 years in two days or two weeks? It generally does not happen, but there is no harm trying.

Even the author of the book *Flow: The Psychology of Optimal Experience* agrees with this. Csikszentmihalyi insists that happiness does not simply happen. It must be prepared for and cultivated by each person, by setting challenges that are neither too demanding nor too simple for one's abilities. Ultimately, contrary to popular notions, the choice to be happy or not lies with us.

This chapter in a nutshell

- To be mentally free of past impressions is to be in the present moment.
- Good or bad, the past is only baggage on the conveyor belt of our mind.

Benefits of meditation off the field

- Meditation gave me a blue print of my mind, and with that came clarity and insight.
- I learnt how to stay in the present and understood the obstacles that come in the way.
- My mind was anchored.
- It improved concentration, focus, performance, awareness and empathy.

- It broke down mental barriers and destroyed fears and insecurities, replacing them *with feelings of self-confidence, energy and joy*.
- My motives were purified.

BENEFITS OF MEDITATION ON THE FIELD

- I kept things simple and stayed tuned to the task on hand.
- I enjoyed myself and yet stayed alert.
- I played out of happiness and not for it.
- I understood the fickle and unreal nature of thoughts.
- I dissociated with unwanted thought processes.
- I learnt to switch on and switch off from thoughts.

On the matter of switching on and switching off, Swami Vivekananda once said, "We put all our energies to concentrate and get attached to one thing; but the other part, though equally difficult, we seldom pay any attention to – the faculty of detaching ourselves at a moment's notice from anything. Both attachment and detachment perfectly developed make a man great and happy."[62]

11. The syncing of two Goliaths

BY UNRAVELLING mysteries and providing scientific explanations for supposedly supernatural phenomena, science has greatly helped us to better understand our world. In the process, it has freed us from superstition. The 'Age of Enlightenment' or simply 'The Age of Reason,' beginning around the 17th and 18th century, was a movement driven by European intellectuals and philosophers. They sought to advance knowledge via scientific means.

William Thompson, also known as Lord Kelvin, an 18th century mathematical physicist and engineer had said, "I am never content, until I have constructed a mechanical model of the subject I am studying. If I have succeeded in making one, I understand, otherwise I do not."[63] However, Einstein believed the rational mind should be a servant to the intuitive mind.

Be that as it may, we are today consumed by a digital world, one that is driven by research, science and technology. It seems to be in our DNA. We need everything rationalised; any theory or idea you posit must have scientific grounding.

It remains to be seen how science will subject 'intuition' to a scientific model. Perhaps it will succeed someday. Volumes of evidence are steadfastly emerging. Science can no longer deny the existence of a consciousness, or at least access to a potential state of being that can reveal treasures that lie hidden away in the mind. Neurologist V S Ramachandran at the University of California (San Diego) talks about a 'God spot' in the temporal lobes of the brain. This is a region that elicited an unusually high response when his research subjects listened to religious words.[64]

When I embarked on the journey of writing this book, I wished to make an effort to elucidate central spiritual perspectives, using a scientific method. Religious indoctrinations, misinterpretations of the scriptures and all the wars fought in the name of God have made the modern generation averse to religious rhetoric. Religion is often discarded and given the stigma of something that has no relevance today. Perhaps there is a need to develop an alternate syntax, a scientific vantage point as it were, to the core of all religions through spirituality.

It would also be interesting, I thought, if the scientific community could explain the pitfalls of excessive individualism, in the way they understand it. Isn't it this idea that we are separate individual entities that causes all the suffering? Isn't it the central psychological plague of our time? Can science throw light on the cause of this feeling of separation?

ENERGY AND SPIRITUALITY

From my exposure to science in school, I remember learning that energy was once undifferentiated and tightly packed into an infinitesimally small space, before the 'Big Bang' – a big explosion that saw the energy expand and result in everything we see around us today. And from that, I'd inferred that we were all one before the world was created.

I did not refer to science before taking on board spiritual values. I heard and read the work of my guide, applied his teachings to my own experience and was instantly drawn to both the teacher and what was being taught. When I began to apply them wholeheartedly, I felt a happier and more confident human being.

But I wanted to understand whether these spiritual ideas have any scientific basis. The concepts professed by all religions – of consciousness, oneness, Nirvana, Mukti, Moksha, Haqiqat, Truth and of an All-pervading presence – do they stand the test of reason? Can they be made easily understandable so that children, who learn complex chemistry and physics equations at grade eight and nine, are not told that they are too young for spirituality?

I enrolled for an online course *on Neurons, Synapses and Brains* by Professor Idan Segev from the Hebrew University of Jerusalem.[65] I learnt how the brain is made up of trillions of nerve cells (neurons) and its interconnections of neural networks that account for everything we do. Francis Crick – The father of DNA and a Nobel Laureate said, "You, your joys and sorrows, your memories and your ambitions, your sense of personal identity are no more than the behaviour of a vast assembly of nerve cells and their associated molecules."[66]

Each nerve cell or neuron (basic building blocks in the brains) at the micro level, generates 'spiking' activity, i.e. it emits an electro-chemical charge or signal. This charge contains information and travels along axons[67] via synapses to reach its destination. This energy or signal that is generated from the spiking activity contains an electric code and has a specific function to execute. Every little action a human being performs, be it moving one's hand, sitting down, talking or standing, is carried in these spikes.

For body movement, the spiking activity occurs in the motor cortex; for images, in the visual cortex; for feelings, in the cerebral cortex and so on. Based on the functions of different regions of the brain, the electrical signals stand for the activity associated with that region. Though they perform different functions, every region of the brain has an identical internal operational mechanism of passing and receiving information.

When we think, visualise or imagine, we create alternative realities inside our head. I was fascinated by how certain computers can process or read signals generated from the spiking activity of neurons. When these computers are plugged to your brain, they can study and interpret your brain's electric language and perform a desired function; this is called Brain Machine Interface.

Neuroscience believes that when you suffer from a disease or any abnormal condition, there could be something wrong with the functioning of the electric circuit or code in the affected region of the brain. To repair the electric circuit is to fix the problem. For this purpose, a machine is implanted – a probe, a pacemaker, an opto-genetics (light) device or other such tool. This is called Deep Brain Simulation. These techniques have made remarkable progress towards curing people suffering from Parkinson's, dystonia and other similar conditions.

The Blue Brain Project attempts to create a virtual model of the entire brain.[68] Through this project, the scientific community will acquire the capacity to simultaneously read billions of signals in real time and understand precisely what happens to our brain in various conditions. Scientists studying these signals will be able to map how the structure of the brain changes in relation to various functions. This could take our understanding of the brain to a whole new level.

I found the *Neurons, Synapses and Brains* course to be very interesting. The unfolding of the inner wiring and working of the brain, as explained by Prof Segev, was so good that I developed a keen interest in anatomy and physiology of the brain. The course helped me arrive at a wonderful insight. I saw that thought, imagination and every little thing we do at the very core is the result of an electric pulse. Since electricity is nothing but a form of energy, we are nothing but energy.

We are energy: A scientific fact

> Mass and energy are both but different manifestations of the same thing.
>
> – *Albert Einstein*[69]

What response do we get when we ask science the 'Who am I' question? Jeff Lieberman, an MIT trained artist and engineer says:

> So who am I? I'm a human being, and I am 33 years old. But if you take a microscope and you look at any part of me, you see cells. I am a community of fifty trillion cells doing a magic dance, but if you look at any one of those cells with an even closer microscope, you see twenty trillion atoms. So I am also a community of a thousand trillion trillion atoms, but when you look at those atoms really up close they fade away, and all you see is energy. And 13.7 billion years ago, at the Big Bang, everything that we've ever found in the universe was one infinitesimal, undifferentiated, pure energy.[70]

When I pose the question 'Who am I' in different contexts, here are the answers I get:

- Who am I in society? – I am the cricketer Ashwath Aiyappa, searching for wealth, fame and status.
- Who am I spiritually? – I am the joy that I experience, my true identity.
- Who am I according to science? – I am nothing but energy.

If I were to sum up, the answer I get from science is energy and from spirituality it is joy. Energy + Joy = Enjoy! Possibly, that's what coaches mean when they say, "Enjoy the game." For when there is joy or happiness it almost always accompanied with an energy or zeal to engage in positive activity, and vice-versa.

So we are *'energy.'* While I intellectually understand this truth, why is it that I do not easily experience it? Why is it that I do not behave like I am energy? Why do I get stuck with society's image of me as an individual with a unique identity, different from everything and everyone around me?

Einstein said, "Thoughts suffer from an optical illusion of consciousness."[71] If he is to be taken seriously, then we again arrive at the same conclusion i.e., that the artificial feeling of separation is raised by thought.

Thoughts and thinking – that have driven modern civilization to such 'great' heights – have also hidden the truth from us. They failed to help us realise that we are energy. Perhaps the process of ordinary thinking can never help us realise this. The time has come to start critically 'thinking about thinking,' for which we need an alternative intelligence.

Masters of the East

In this age of self-preservation, we must remember that there were great souls, the real 'cool dudes' of humanity whose lives and words still hold relevance today.

Be it Buddha, Christ, Ramakrishna Paramahansa, Nizamudin Auliya, Swami Vivekananda or Gandhi, they all have certain things in common – they spoke the language of unity, they saw no division and their dreams went beyond themselves. They were filled with love and compassion for mankind and above all, they were fearless. They had all seen the macrocosm in the microcosm. As Swami Vivekananda so eloquently stated, "I felt that the sun, moon, space, time, ether and all had been reduced to a homogeneous mass."[72]

Perhaps these teachers had a direct experience of being energy. This direct experience is what they called Realization, Moksha, Haqiqat or Truth. When the veil is removed from the mind, it sees its true nature. Previously erected boundaries that defined the separate identity crumbled to fill one's being with an unexplainable bliss.

Science and Spirituality

Jeff Lieberman elaborates on energy and spirituality:

> When we look at monks and nuns who have meditated or prayed for thousands of hours we see remarkable shifts on their brain scans. Trillions of neural connections have changed configuration. Along with this quantifiable, objective change in the operating system of the brain, they describe a feeling of undifferentiated, infinite, oneness. To me that sounds like they are having the direct experience of being energy. Enlightenment science and enlightenment engineering would study these ancient technologies

of prayer and meditation as data sets to understand what has to change in the structure of a human brain for a human being to understand that they are energy directly. We still have no idea how much modern technology could completely change our ability to understand that. Maybe it's possible that within our lifetimes we could eradicate human suffering.

When you let go of individual survival, all of your priorities change because you actually see the entire world as your body. You see the suffering of others as your own suffering and you want to help. What if seven billion of us did that?

Maybe the one thing that keeps us from actually solving all of the other problems in the world is this persistent, flawed thought that we are separate from the world. Maybe it's time we change our minds.[73]

When our brain attains a certain structure, it gives us a direct experience of an aspect of reality that is otherwise hidden from our normal view, an experience that irreversibly transforms character. I think the feeling of being energy is truly the purest form of being in the present, devoid of conflict. Sri M states:

One aspect of reality has been explored and exploited to the optimum level – the outside world, which mostly the left brain, the rational, practical brain deals with. The other aspect of reality, the inner which the intuitive, right brain is concerned with, has somehow been neglected except perhaps in the fields of arts and aesthetics.

The inner aspect is what the science of yoga deals with. When these and other hitherto untouched centres in the brain or psyche if you prefer to call it, are activated, the human being enters an extraordinary world of infinite power, majesty and grandeur wherein the inner and the outer become one and the human transcends his human-ness to become divine.[74]

Now let's look at a person, not just any person and more importantly not a saint or a monk, but a scientist. She's a neuro-anatomist from

Harvard University, who had a serendipitous encounter with her right brain.

Jill Bolte Taylor and her stroke of insight

On the morning of 10th December 1996, Dr Jill Bolte Taylor, the author of the book *My Stroke of Insight*, had a haemorrhage. A blood vessel exploded in the left half of her brain. Transitioning between pain and wonder, she watched her brain completely deteriorate in its ability to process all information. She could not walk, talk, read, write or recall any of her life. Her left-brain and the important functions it performs had shut down. But her right brain was functioning and she experienced it in all its splendour.

The human brain is made up of two hemispheres – the left and the right.[75] The two hemispheres are separate from one another and also process data differently. They communicate via a highway of information transfer, the corpus callosum,[76] which is made up of some 300 million axonal fibres. When the left and the right hemispheres function normally, they produce a seamless perception of the world.

Explaining how the right brain works, Dr Bolte said in a TED talk:

> Our right human hemisphere is all about this present moment. It's all about "right here, right now." Our right hemisphere, it thinks in pictures and it learns kinaesthetically through the movement of our bodies. Information, in the form of energy, streams in simultaneously through all of our sensory systems and then it explodes into this enormous collage of what this present moment looks like, what this present moment smells like and tastes like, what it feels like and what it sounds like. I am an energy-being connected to the energy all around me through the consciousness of my right hemisphere.[77]

On how the left brain works, she said:

> My left hemisphere – our left hemisphere – is a very different place. Our left hemisphere thinks linearly and methodically. Our left hemisphere is all about the past and it's all about the future. Our left hemisphere is designed to take that enormous collage of the present moment and start picking out details, details and

> more details about those details. It then categorizes and organizes all that information, associates it with everything in the past we've ever learned, and projects into the future all of our possibilities.
>
> But perhaps most important, it's that little voice that says to me, "I am. I am." And as soon as my left hemisphere says to me "I am," I become separate. I become a single solid individual, separate from the energy flow around me and separate from you. And this was the portion of my brain that I lost on the morning of my stroke.[78]

Without the left brain, and the stroke spreading to her right arm, she had trouble performing the simple task of making a phone call for help – and it took her over an hour to do so. She described how she felt in the ambulance on the way to hospital:

> I felt my spirit surrender. And in that moment, I knew that I was no longer the choreographer of my life. And either the doctors rescue my body and give me a second chance at life, or this was perhaps my moment of transition.[79]

Talking about her right-brain experience, she said:

> [I]t was beautiful there. Imagine what it would be like to be totally disconnected from your brain chatter that connects you to the external world. So here I am in this space, and my job – and any stress related to my job – it was gone. And I felt lighter in my body. And imagine all of the relationships in the external world and any stressors related to any of those – they were gone. And I felt this sense of peacefulness. And imagine what it would feel like to lose 37 years of emotional baggage! Oh! I felt euphoria – euphoria.[80]

She recounted her situation on regaining consciousness:

> Because I could not identify the position of my body in space, I felt enormous and expansive, like a genie just liberated from her bottle. And my spirit soared free, like a great whale gliding through the sea of silent euphoria. Nirvana. I found Nirvana. And if I have

found Nirvana and I'm still alive, then everyone who is alive can find Nirvana.[81]

In losing the left portion of her brain, she lost all identification with her 'little self' or her ego and stumbled upon a great inner treasure, all by accident. She lost her sense of personal identity – that she was Dr Jill Bolte Taylor, neuro-anatomist/Intellectual, and being free of that identity allowed her to have the transforming experience of oneness. This is scary when it happens by means of a stroke, but when brought about over years of proper spiritual guidance and practice, there are no such dangers to life. This is similar to batsmen who tune their reflexes to play fast bowling (which others might consider dangerous).

Dr Taylor's experience is so significant because as a brain scientist, she walks us through her spiritual experience using scientific language and finally refers to it as 'Nirvana.' She uses words like enormous, expansive, euphoria and energy. But ultimately, words don't matter as much as the 'state of being' these words describe. Her experience appears identical to the ultimate spiritual experience of unity or oneness described by spiritual giants of the world.

Though the paths are very different, the final experience points undeniably towards the existence of a potential life-transforming reality sitting inside the inter circuitries of our right brain, waiting to be had.

In fact science is catching up at a great speed and as evidence steadily emerges, the day is not distant when spirituality and its principles of unity will be taught as a subject in classrooms the world over. That to me will be the 'Syncing of the two Goliaths' (i.e., the left and right brains, science and spirituality).

LEFT-RIGHT LEFT-RIGHT

If one walks with only one leg, how far can one go?

For instance when batting, the importance of factors such as balance, weight transfer, shot selection and timing become stored knowledge after years of practice. This constitutes the working of the left-brain. The left hemisphere being methodical and logical in nature, probably believes that everything can be explained and controlled. I call this the scientific half and it is very much needed.

Even if we master the skills of the game, results are not guaranteed. This is perhaps where, if the right brain gets triggered, it can offer its intuitive abilities to bring out one's true potential. So why not develop both left and right in equal measure?

The right in all religions

Several religions emphasise prayers, meditative techniques, devotional singing, dancing and glorifying the Almighty. Maybe they are merely prescribing psychological exercises that focus the mind and bring peace, while freeing the mind of lop-sided left-brain thinking. Perhaps the aim is to organically change the structure of our brain to move away from all self-centred ideas, and towards the *intuitive experience of unity*.

That there is so much suffering caused in the name of religion is evidence that its custodians have yet to succeed. Be that as it may, the left-brain on its own may find it extremely hard to romance an idea of a 'God.' When you subject the popular idea of God to logic, it does not survive the scrutiny. Eminent journalist Mr Arun Shourie's book *Does He [God] Know a Mother's Heart* is one such inquiry that is matchless.

The feeling of love, energy and sheer awesomeness that Dr Taylor described gives us an idea of the power sitting inside us, untapped. To excel, we need to engage it. The right brain experience is not entirely uncommon to sportspersons. On some days, we slip into the oxymoronic state of intense yet relaxed concentration, the zone.

When I bat out of joy and love, I call it soul batting – batting for its own sake, free of all burdens. My 'zone' experiences were the happiest moments of my cricketing life. Unfortunately I spent only 0.5% of my cricketing life in that zone.

Soul performance

Batting can be like poetry. When touched by words of a poet or the melodious voice of a singer, our minds are instantly transported to another world. We feel healed as joy wells up in our hearts. It's almost as if the music or the words have pierced through the dense jungle of nerve cells in the brain, to reach its source.

I would find that dot balls lost their meaning, pressure lost its meaning, the need to impress or to be someone was absent. Runs seemed to flow very easily when it was made unimportant; long hours in the sun seemed to go by effortlessly, and my profession suddenly seemed fun, like one big party. This should not be confused with recklessness or carelessness, but a state in which there is no fear of failure. You cannot try to get into that state; it happens only when the ego steps aside.

Invariably, coaches say, "play freely", or "play from your heart". How is this to be done? What does this even mean? There is a difference between playing from the heart and playing from the mind. I think when coaches say 'play freely,' they mean, play from a state that is free of prejudice, of self-imposed limitation and of even technique at those critical moments.

I'm sure if you go back in your career and look closely, you would have played this way on several occasions. We just have to understand the triggers that get one into that sort of a zone, and try to internalise those triggers so that we more routinely play from that state.

Knowing now the intrinsic nature of each hemisphere of the brain, we can easily identify the part to which a particular thought or feeling belongs. And accordingly, we can associate our minds with positive thoughts that will allow our minds to expand. We can now choose which parts of our brain will dominate our lives, according to the situation we find ourselves in.

The ABCs of counter-thinking

What helped me overcome the anxiety associated with the ups and downs of a sporting career were thought processes that were both logical and spiritual. They acted as counter-thoughts every time insecure feelings attacked. Here are three examples:

1. I will be happy for my rival's success, as the universe/god/energy/nature, call it what you may, has handed it to him. He must be worthy of it, I accept it and I am happy for him. My time will also come, I don't have to worry, so let me celebrate his success.
2. All human beings have emerged from the same source and now that I know this, I will not listen to the ego's voice – it is out to trick me again, and I must be eternally vigilant. I refuse to give such negative deflating thoughts any importance; instead I will starve them to death.
3. My success depends on my abilities and actions, not others' failures.

All the above affirmations engage both brain centres. The need of the hour is to develop both the right and left parts of the brain, i.e. whole brain development. Wouldn't it be nice if we had a brain that has a healthy mix of the following:

- Intelligence and innocence
- Intuition and reason
- Detachment and attachment
- Creativity and logic
- Calculation and risk-taking
- Caution and abandon

Such a brain sees only opportunity and never failure.

Summary: A brain map

The left brain works through:

- Assessment
- Analysis
- Evaluation
- Judgment
- Examination
- Calculation
- Details
- Logic
- Organization
- Science
- Facts
- Sequence
- Method
- Linearity
- Language
- Personality

The right brain works through:

- Creativity
- Imagination
- Intuition
- Spirituality
- Philosophy
- Feelings
- Symbols
- Religion
- Randomness

12. The Science of meditation

WE SEEM TO instinctively know that meditation is beneficial for one's well-being. It is an age old spiritual practice associated with most religions of the world. Numerous scientific studies have highlighted several advantages of meditation, including:

- Lowered blood pressure
- Decreased stress
- Alleviated symptoms of depression, anxiety, pain & insomnia
- Enhanced immune system
- Improved quality of life
- Better emotion regulation

Meditation not only improves one's health, but research has also proved its profound impact on the brain and its functionality:

- Increased grey matter
- Increased attention and concentration
- Improved working memory
- Better information processing

Neuroplasticity: Our plastic brain

I spoke about neuroscience in the previous chapter. In this chapter, I will delve into neuroplasticity, also called neuronal plasticity. Until fairly recently, scientists believed that the brain, once fully developed, could not change. If any damage or trauma occurred to a part of the brain, the related functions were considered to be gone forever.

But research has now shown that the brain is 'plastic' – that it can change. Neurons are quite capable (when sufficiently coaxed) of changing the way they communicate with each other. The more plastic a brain, the more its grasping ability.

A child's brain is like a sponge. In contrast, an adult's brain was likened to a sieve. As a result of the sponge-like plasticity, children are normally able to learn instruments or pick up new skills faster than adults. However, evidence has emerged to show that even an ageing brain is capable of new feats, though it requires a little extra effort. This means that we can change our brains and thus change ourselves. At any age!

Practice makes perfect

When we engage or repeat a movement constantly, as our coaches so often make us do in practice, it leads to changes in our brain. To illustrate this, let's consider a study in which a group of people was taught how to juggle, and asked to regularly practice for three months. At the end of three months, scans of their brain were taken. Scientists noticed marked changes in the grey matter levels in areas of the brain that were important for detecting visual motion.

This means if a violinist has practiced over 10,000 hours, the associated region in the brain (motor cortex) changes. It increases and reinforces synaptic[82] connections and establishes pathways to make the necessary movements reflexive and effortless.

Research on meditation

Prompted by this finding, Dr Sara Lazar (a neuroscientist and a meditation/yoga practitioner herself) decided to conduct a neuro-imaging study to see if any such change was possible with meditation.[83] She recruited people and divided them into two groups – those who meditated for roughly half an hour every day and those who did not.

The results of the MRI (Magnetic Resonance Imaging) scans showed more grey matter in several regions of the brains of those who meditated, as opposed to those who did not. Among the regions, the pre-frontal cortex is particularly important because it is responsible for working memory, executive decision-making, and the performance of vital day-to-day functions.

The study found that 50-year-olds in the first group who practiced meditation had as much cortex in the prefrontal region as the 25 year olds who did not meditate. This strongly suggests that meditation slows down or prevents age related decline in cortical structures.

This study had its share of criticism; those opposed to the findings said the long term benefits accrued by the meditators could be the result of continuous practice. Therefore, another study was conducted, in which non-meditators were divided into two groups. MRI scans of the brains of both groups were taken. One was put through an eight-week meditation-based stress reduction program, whereas the other group was not.

In those who meditated, a remarkable increase was found in both size and quantity of grey matter in the regions of the brain associated with functions such as learning, memory, emotion, compassion and the fight/ flight response. What's interesting is that the change in grey matter correlated to the change in stress. In other words, the more stress reduction people reported, the smaller the amygdala[84] became. For those who meditated, nothing had changed in their environment. In Dr Lazar's words, "They still had their stressful jobs, all the difficult people in their lives were still being difficult and the economy still sucked, yet the amygdala got smaller and they were reporting less stress." This shows that the amygdala is representing the change in people's response or relationship to the environment."

Dr Lazar concluded, "The other thing that the study shows us is that it wasn't just that people were saying, 'Oh I feel better' or that it was placebo response or that they were trying to please us, but they were actual neurobiological reasons to why they were saying they felt less stressed."

Overall, these changes helped the brain not only spiritually (as most of the participants reported feeling more compassion and peace), but also cognitively and emotionally. Therefore, spiritual practices impact the whole brain and not just parts of it. The more one studies the brain, the more it appears that the brain is wired for spiritual experience.

Given this undeniable spirituality, how should we set and accomplish mundane goals?

13. Goal keeping

A PERFECTION OF means, and confusion of aims, seems to be our main problem.

– *Albert Einstein*

Confusion arises when we psychologically create a distance or separation between the process and the goal. When we separate the two, we essentially tell ourselves:

- I am here and I have to get there.
- Today I am not worthy, but if I reach there, I will become worthy.

The 'I have to get there' part subtly implies a rejection of 'the now' as the mind looks towards the future for fulfilment. All striving is then undertaken from feelings of lack, with the hope that the realisation of the goal will remove it.

Why can't we be happy and seek to improve? Why must the process of getting or seeking be one that creates disharmony? Can we not accept our lot in life and then strive for more? The point is, the process of acquiring does not always have to be a bitter or a desperate one. But if our brains are wired to let happiness in only when a goal is attained, all thinking becomes inseparably linked to result.

Goal setting in my view must involve both a *macro* and a *micro* picture. The macro aspect of goal setting *is meant to only set direction,* just as you know the destination before you set out on a journey.

Say I decide to go to Ooty from Bengaluru. The goal is Ooty – and so the direction in which my vehicle will move is set. Once that is done, it would be foolish if I obsess about reaching Ooty and not enjoy the journey. The macro picture in this case is the destination (Ooty) and the micro picture is the process of driving and revelling in the sights en-route. *For is it not the journey that delivers you to the destination*?

Having an ambition to become something or someone is natural. All the greats advise us to dream big, set high goals and take risks. But you will never enjoy the journey if you are constantly worrying about the destination, or the millions of things that could go wrong on the way. Just dump those scary blinkers and keep going.

Nothing really exists besides the process, besides the now. Think about it. Right now you are reading this book. If it hasn't put you to sleep and if you're not bored, you're probably quite interested. Your mind is completely engrossed and you aren't worrying about the past or the future. That's all it means to enjoy the process.

Some goal-keeping tips or pointers to remember:

- Do what you enjoy doing (when you do what you love, certain qualities of mind naturally come about such as concentration, energy and perseverance).
- Be passionate about the process and dispassionate about the result.
- Ensure motives are continually checked.

I was now excited to put all that I had learnt post the KPL debacle to the test.

Testing times – The Times Shield

I loved playing in the Times Shield in Mumbai, as one gets an opportunity to play against some of the top players in India. As someone who had yet to play in the Ranji Trophy, it was always challenging for me. I remember a coach saying, "If you score a century in the Times 'A' Division, it is equal if not more than a first class hundred. Each of the teams that participate recruits the best players from India, and not just Mumbai or Maharashtra."

Both the D Y Patil grounds were excellent venues to play cricket. My first opportunity was in a match against Western Railway.[85] Again, prematch jitters and negative thoughts returned to haunt me. Here are a couple of them:

- Will I get a chance to play, as the team is packed with current state and ex Ranji-players and I am the only one who is not a current or ex Ranji player?
- What if I get a chance and don't perform? Then I am sure to be dropped, because there are three wicket-keepers in this team.

But this time round my mind reacted differently to these thoughts. It understood what these *'prank thoughts'* were up to, and was able to smile at them and say, "Well tried." This new mind stated, "Whatever happens I will accept boldly with a smile, as it will be for the best." All the meditation had helped me better understand my mental strengths and weaknesses.

The 'prank thoughts' were to do with things that I had no control over. What I could control was my mental preparation leading up to the game. I filled my head with all the right thoughts and ideas of how I wanted to approach my innings. I knew if I was selected I would play as a batsman and not as a wicket-keeper.

I had by now understood that I always did well when I kept thoughts of result away. All the false shots and hasty decisions in my life that led to failures and disappointments were in some way connected to fear. I was a worrier and not a warrior.

The most important thing was to insulate myself from the burden of outcome and the attention seeking quality of my mind. I had to accordingly prepare myself by doing three things:

- Ensure I enjoyed my batting.
- Counter both stray thoughts from my mind and nullify sledges delivered by opponent fieldsmen.
- Keep things simple and stay in the present by constantly returning focus to the task on hand.

Moreover, I constantly drilled the following thoughts into my mind before that game:

1. I do not care if I get out early. I do not care if we lose. I will bat for the love of batting and not for a pat on my back from my coach, teammate or anyone else (ironically, this thinking helped me perform and the team benefitted).
2. Maybe today everyone sees me as a failure, but nobody has seen tomorrow. Like me, my opponents are mere mortals, and apart from the Almighty nobody has the right to judge me. So don't sweat over what people say.
3. All I have to do is play just one ball each time. No matter what the situation, no bowler will simultaneously bowl two balls at me.
4. Even my mother can play one ball.

I internalised these points as much as I could. I then picked up my bat, turned the lights off, closed my eyes and imagined myself playing a few overs. I imagined various scenarios where fieldsmen were mocking me for not being able to score runs quickly or my teammates saying, "How slowly this fellow plays." I also visualised myself scoring runs freely and getting very excited and happy about the way I was batting.

In each of these scenarios, my only goal was to play 'Just one ball at a time.' All other thoughts did not deserve any importance. *The only pressure I allowed my mind to nurse was the responsibility of staying focused on the coming delivery.*

And my mind seemed quite confident, comfortable and happy with this new idea. I felt confident and assured of my chances on the morrow. I realised much later that by doing this I had made *the process the goal, the end and also the result.* All focus and energy was shifted to the journey and away from worrisome thoughts of the destination. In a corner of my mind, the macro picture was to play till the end of the innings. I was mentally wiring myself to focus on the process till the last ball was bowled. *I felt this was a perfect marriage between the destination and the journey.*

Match day: The game

I will share with you my diary entry on that day, Nov 17, 2009.

> Before walking into bat after a light lunch, I did nine rounds of slow breathing. It really helped me get centred. After I went into bat, all I did was to play one ball and never bothered about runs or anything. I was at peace out there in the middle. Every time my mind wandered into the future or the past I never gave that thought any importance. I kept reinforcing my 'just one ball' mantra and bringing my mind back. Sometimes, when I felt that my mind was getting away, I requested the Almighty to save me from distracting thoughts.
>
> I even hit three massive on-drive sixes. Towards the end of the day, it got quite difficult; I began to cough profusely, but that peace of mind and ball-to-ball focus never left me. I would watch the ball closely and play my shot with as much care and presence. My fitness held up well and I batted till the end of the day. Whoever got out at the other end, it never disturbed my peace of mind and focus.
>
> All this is certainly a result of my meditation. It is the first time ever I had this peace of mind for prolonged periods during a game.

> I thoroughly enjoyed all the challenges out there. I am 14 shy of my hundred and there are two wickets in hand, and I am certain that tomorrow will be great. I feel like I have finally arrived.

I batted for six hours and completed my century the following day (my birthday), and ended up with 113 not out off 230 balls. The team score was 280. We won that game outright, but on the last day while fielding I broke my little finger.

PROCESS AS GOAL AND COUNTER THINKING

During this particular game and other matches that followed, I achieved best results every time I successfully employed this method.

For instance, when runs were scarce, I often felt a rowdy urge to whack the ball. But then I would overrule that impulse saying, "It's just a thought, I don't have to act on it, I will be rewarded if I stick to my method." Invariably, soon afterwards I would get a ball onto my pads that I would dispatch to the fence. It almost felt as if the heavens were rewarding me for successfully fending off devilish urges.

On an average through my cricketing life, I found that if I played 30 balls, I normally scored at least 15 runs. The bowlers are bound to bowl at least four boundary balls in 30 deliveries, and if you have reasonable skill you are sure to also pick up singles. So if you maintain ball-to-ball focus and not let the events of the previous ball overlap or impact shot selection for the current ball, runs are never a problem.

Sometimes, a bowler or fielder would walk up and say, "You are not going to make it, you know that right," or, "Bowling to you is a waste of time," or some other nasty thing. Once a bowler even said, "Can I have your ex-girlfriend's phone number, she is single now right, I want to have a go at her." I smiled it off and responded, "Man that is nasty, you know that," and continued batting.

When a fielder sledges you, he does not hate you, he is simply doing his job. At the end of the day, the same fielder will smile and congratulate you. The trick is to not take it personally, which of course is easier said than done.

Players often chase imaginary fears that could be triggered by a comment from a teammate or a coach. The fears could pertain to information about the pitch, prowess of an opponent, their own skill level and sometimes also their positions in the playing 11.

One reason a player's game magically elevates to another level on reaching a milestone is simply that he feels relief and peace, and then plays from that state of security. The more I practiced this technique, thoughts that initially bothered me would just disappear, and I began to look forward to the next ball. The more balls I played with that attitude, the more I would notice the chatter becoming less intense, both inside my mind and outside.

Fielders would be simply standing around waiting for me to get out and I was on top now. I easily continued to play just one ball each time. Shots began to flow from a deeper, quieter space within my mind. When I passed the first milestone (half century) I heard voices as though coming from a distance, and realised that I had done something important. Then came the second part, which was nothing but executing the first part again. Even when I was on top, I kept reminding myself of the process and the thinking I had employed to get there.

There is the danger of excess joy that can cause an error. Everyone will tell you that too much sadness causes depression, but likewise too much happiness also causes disturbances. To be calm is to be in control.

At times when my ego began to get away, I would take a moment and thank the universe. I would say:

> *Thank you for this very opportunity* and for everything else you have done for me, and for focusing my mind correctly. But my duty is incomplete. I have to stay with the same focus till the last ball is bowled and if you don't help me it cannot be done. Please help me stay in the present and keep things simple. Everything else I leave to you, I will accept any outcome.

Immediately, *when I showed genuine gratitude, the ego would step aside.* How would a Buddha approach the game, I would ask myself. I found that when one stays in the present and plays out of happiness, *one truly experiences God's pleasure*.

I used the same method to make 68 in the finals of the Times 'B' division. I was nursing a bruised ankle and had failed to make runs in the first innings. I felt all my efforts would be discounted if I failed again in such an important game.

In preparation for my next innings, I did my rounds of focusing on my breath, and walked in to bat feeling joy. Tactics, strategy – nothing mattered. Everything was happening in slow motion and the ball repeatedly found the meat of my bat. It was without a doubt an innings where my shot selection was driven more by intuition than anything else.

We won the Times Shield that year and our team was promoted to 'A' division. In 2011, I got another unbeaten hundred employing the same method against a very good bowling attack. This was after recovering from a string of six injuries to both my shoulders, my knees, ankle and two finger injuries. After that innings I felt extremely satisfied and relieved. I no longer doubted my abilities and lost all feelings of inferiority. I guess I just wanted to know deep down that I was good enough. I felt vindicated and began to feel the obsession with cricket wearing off. I was able to think of a life beyond it, and strangely this felt like a victory.

When the process and the goal are separated

As we have seen, almost all mental storms are brought about by a fear that we may not obtain a certain outcome. Expectation, the need to impress or look good, jealousy, lack of confidence, anger, shame, the need to control what another person thinks of you, and almost every other conceivable pressure that pulls the mind down, are in some way connected to reward.

When the process becomes the goal, the mind is relaxed and the brain is not tensed. If the mind understands that all it needs to do is play one ball, then you've successfully broken the negative chain of thoughts. *But the mind first needs to be coaxed out of result-oriented thinking, before it becomes stabilised in process-oriented values. Like anything else, this requires practice.*

I want to talk of another aspect of goal setting in the next chapter. But before we go there, let me summarise the benefits of making the process the goal:

- It enables the mind to stay in the present.
- Lofty goals that can cause pressure and seem impossible to achieve, are broken down and greatly simplified, and the mind begins to believe that it can easily perform.
- Simplification of the task and clear communication with self also brings clarity.
- Counter thoughts/affirmations are assigned, and act as anchors that keep the mind focused, and maintain vigilance against negative thought processes.

- Staying focused increases one's chance of success.
- Redefines conventional meanings of success and failure – success and failure lie in effort and commitment to process and not result.

The irony

Though we had won the Times Shield and mentally at least I had finally become "fit," I returned to Bengaluru with two injuries. My left index finger had dislocated (I had taped it and fielded), and my right ankle was badly twisted during the final. I was unable to go all out and prepare for the Bengaluru league – the ankle eventually took over a year to recover. The irony was none too amusing, for up until that point I was known to be physically super-fit but mentally unfit. Now that I had sorted out my mental issues to a great extent, my body was falling apart.

It was very frustrating and *I began to hold myself responsible for something I had no control over*. And instead of ruling myself out, I played matches without fully recovering and that only made things worse. This brings me to another aspect of goal-setting and of life itself.

14. Stop it you control freak

EVERYTHING IS determined by forces over which we have no control. It is determined for the insect as well as for the star. Human beings, vegetables or cosmic dust we all dance to a mysterious tune, intoned in the distance by a mysterious piper.

– *Albert Einstein*[86]

While we don't have total control over everything that happens, we can control our responses. I want to illustrate this with a short story.

Two boys have toiled long and hard for an examination. They have burnt the midnight oil and acquired the necessary knowledge to excel. They both rely on a bus to take them from their village to the exam hall, an hour away. The exam is slated for 10 am. The bus normally arrives at 8am. On exam day, the bus has a flat tyre and reaches the village by 9:30am. One of the two boys panics. He begins to curse his luck, spends all his time and thoughts thinking about the consequences of being late.

In other words, without realising it, *he begins to hold himself responsible for what happened,* when he had nothing to do with it. Nevertheless he blames himself. While this boy frets, the other boy listens to music, enjoys the sights, strikes conversations with fellow passengers and generally enjoys himself. For whatever reason, he has a different take. He knows that there was nothing he could do about the bus coming late and reasons, "All that happens probably happens for the best."

The bus finally reaches the exam hall. Both boys exit the bus at *the same time after enduring similar circumstances, but with very different attitudes.* One gets off the bus with a tensed, stressed and agitated mind. The other is positive and is somehow still looking forward to making the most of the time he has left.

See the difference? Once you hop onto the bus of life, never forget to enjoy the ride no matter how bumpy. Remember you cannot control all factors en route – a puncture, traffic jams, the driver making a mistake, or the bus coming late. Say a prayer and wish with all your heart that all goes well. Accept the highs and lows with equanimity.

To be free, you must be absolutely vulnerable. You must be comfortable with the thought that anything can happen. Embrace uncertainty. Make yourself absolutely available for the moment, knowing fully well that anything can happen.

Merging process and goal

Those of us who have played sport long enough understand through experience that, though there certainly exists a connection between effort and success, the relationship is not strictly linear. You cannot say with certainty that if I put in 'x' effort, I will obtain a 'y' result. This is because obtaining a particular result generally depends on many factors that are outside our control.

In an ideal world, the relationship between effort and success would be direct and tangible. Yes, when one puts in effort and prepares well, he places himself in a great position to succeed. But that still does not guarantee it. In fact *uncertainty* is the only constant factor.

Taking the example of cricket. No matter how well you prepare as a batsman, you may get a wicket that is under-prepared or the bowler may bowl an absolutely unplayable ball. You may get a bad decision, suffer an injury, or the match may be called off due to rain. There is a whole list of uncontrollable factors that could go against you. Likewise, these factors could go in your favour on many occasions.

The book *The Success Equation* by Michael Mauboussin demolishes a lot of myths. It is a very good read to better understand the role of luck and skill from a scientific viewpoint. Mr Mauboussin's work explains that in today's highly competitive climate, *improving skills makes results more reliant on luck.* In his book, he says, "Greater skill does not decrease the dependence on luck, it only increases it."[87]

Mr Mauboussin makes two broad points:

- In several sports, performance depends on many interacting factors. In such sports, batting averages over the years have always reduced.
- In sports where performance doesn't depend on interacting factors, performance has consistently improved (eg swimming and athletics, in which performances are measured against a clock).

Mr Bauboussin quotes the work of Stephen Jay Gould, an evolutionary biologist at Harvard University and a keen baseball enthusiast. Mr Gould wrote an essay to explain why no major league baseball player could average more than .400 or equal Ted Williams's score of .406 that was set in 1941. Cricket and baseball being very similar sports, the same applies to cricket. Don Bradman's average of 99.94 that was set way back in 1948 still stands today and seems likely to never be surpassed. Does that mean players of eras gone by are way better than the present lot? Mr Mauboussin says:

> Gould considered several conventional explanations, including more night games, demanding travel, improved fielding, and more extensive use of relief pitching. None checked out. Maybe Williams was some sort of freak player, Gould thought, better than all of those who came before him as well as all of those who followed. That's implausible, he concluded, because in every sport where performance is measured versus a clock, including swimming and running, athletes have improved. Baseball players are better than they were in the past: faster, stronger, more fit, and better trained.
>
> So how do we solve the mystery of the vanishing .400 hitter? The best approach is to set up a simple model that explains how greater skill can lead to a greater reliance on luck. We'll then apply our model to other realms to see if it explains what we see there. In each case, we'll see that luck has more sway even as participants hone their skill. It's the paradox of skill.[88]

Gould pointed out that over decades, players from different nationalities began playing the game, leading to an expanded pool of talent. With the advent of professional training techniques, performances improved across the league. As a result, the gap in skill between the top player and the lower ranked players became narrower over time.

Hence, in the absence of luck, this makes it harder for any batter to significantly outperform others. This 'paradox of skill' is explained using 'The Jars of Success.' There are two jars:

1. Skills jar
2. Luck jar

As skill has improved since Ted Williams's era (1940s), the Skills Jar shows a significant change over the decades, while the luck jar remains the same. The 'luck factor' is considered to be the same in 1940 as it is today.

> That the bell curve in the skill jar gets skinnier over time while the bell curve in the luck jar remains the same, means that as skill improves for the population, luck becomes more important in determining results. On average, players have greater skill today than they did in years past but their outcomes are more tied to luck. This extends to other realms as well.[89]

Despite all the preparation and toil one puts in to maximise skill through hours of practice, there is always an element of chance. One cannot afford to think he owns the outcome. It's not like a transaction in a retail shop, where you pay 20 rupees and are sure to get something in return for the money.

Ideally speaking

As much as possible, systems must be put in place with the aid of science and technology to reduce injustices. Right from selection of players to on-field incidents, there must be established criteria and transparency to ensure fairness. Several technologies introduced in both cricket and tennis have removed human errors. But these technologies are available only at the highest levels of the sport. Everyone else has to contend with systems subject to human fallibility.

Those with access to powerful lobbies are sometimes able to find a way to linearise their effort and reward equation. Outcomes that depend on luck for others, for them depend on the use of contacts and networks.

A bulletproof mind

Since results depend more on luck in highly skilled environments, the link between effort and result in our minds must be completely severed. This is a tall order because all of us heavily invest effort in some agenda or the other. From an investment we always expect returns and this makes us feel a sense of *ownership* of the reward.

Imagine a scenario in which a result-oriented mind was to fail altogether, even after repeated attempts. Think of how betrayed, rejected or let down it would feel. Think of the drain such a mind would experience, what a deep scar it could leave. It would be as if the mind were in a car crash. For such a mind to rehabilitate itself would be an extremely difficult task.

A good friend of mine and an ex-Ranji player once began removing his clothes in response to a customary taunt during a match. Though an excellent player, he just could not handle the rejection of not getting picked, and it came out in a very strange manner.

But name one athlete who has not failed! When success comes, the happiness is extreme, which too will throw the mind off balance. Too much of anything is bad. Moderation is key.

Despite our best preparation and advice that any book or teacher may offer, setbacks are inevitable. So it is good to develop strong shoulders and backs. If we repeatedly succumb to disappointment and allow it to make us bitter, we merely ready the ground for the next upheaval. Every angry reaction is bound to bring about another.

When we cannot accept what has happened, we stress and actually go against the whole of nature. There is no point trying to change the present or past. Instead, just witness it as if you are a stranger in your own life. No one, and I mean no one, has ever succeeded in changing the past; you can only learn from it.

When we say, and we often do say it, "The outcome is not in my hands," whether we like it or not, we are admitting to the mysterious nature of how things unfold in this world. We may call it good luck, bad luck, chance, God, grace, providence or whatever else and move on with our lives. So we must enable our minds to develop qualities that make our minds more process friendly.

A quick recap:

- Sacrifice feelings of ownership and responsibility towards outcomes (uncontrollables).
- Let go of control and embrace vulnerability.
- Control what we can (effort, motive and preparation).
- In case of adverse outcomes, wholeheartedly accept it. Don't feel guilty of failure.
- *To become mentally bulletproof, one should become indifferent or dispassionate to result and very passionate about the process.*

I can name three quality batsmen who probably put in as much effort and scored as many runs if not more than any of their counterparts, but never got a national call. They were up against the calibre of Dravid, Laxman and Ganguly. Now how could they control that? Well they couldn't. They can either choose to accept it and move on, or not.

> Remember that not getting what you want is sometimes a wonderful stroke of luck.
>
> – *The Dalai Lama*

15. Fear of failure

LIVING WITH FEAR and using it as a means to drive action, consciously or otherwise, has become a way of life. There are many who frighten themselves into performing. I am no exception. It exhausted me and took a huge toll on my body and mind.

To remedy this, one must take on his fear head on. Imagine the worst-case scenario, the worst possible thing that could happen to you and become mentally comfortable with it. Do not run away. Prepare for the worst but hope for the best. This is similar to 'progressive muscle relaxation' where you tense the muscle to a point from where it is forced to then relax.

Consciously, take all your negative thoughts to the extreme instead of constantly trying to evade them. Live them out in your head and let those thoughts know you don't fear them. Once you get to know its true nature, you can overcome it.

Negative thoughts are actually weak. They have no business to be in our minds. They live in the dark like rodents and are scared. Light is therefore the best disinfectant; the light of awareness and spiritual understanding in this case.

Sri M once told me, "If you are in a room alone with a cobra, you cannot afford to make sudden movements, it will strike you. If you want to conquer it you must first get to know it, try and understand it. For which you need to be calm and patient."

I always tried to avoid negative thoughts and they constantly chased me. I felt guilty and agitated every time they appeared in my mind. But when I stopped running and faced them, I was able to understand and deal with them in a better way.

Pain and pleasure

Every time I failed in a match, I could not be alone with myself. I would either go for a movie, or to a friend's place or order food and eat incessantly, all to distract myself from the hurt that I was feeling. By doing this I never addressed the real issue that was causing the pain. I always brushed it under the carpet.

What would happen if every time you spilt coffee, you'd just let it be without cleaning it? Over time, you would have a floor filled with stains and the sight of it would get unbearable. Cleaning the mess would be a painful and time-consuming task. In the same way, restoring a mind that has been badly broken by circumstance and false conditioning to its original state is a monumental undertaking.

We will do well to have a mental routine in place. This could take the form of writing down the day's activities and being as objective as possible in our analysis of it. Alternatively, we could examine our minds with meditation or a breathing technique. It could be a prayer or anything else that helps you relax and let go.

Whatever be your choice, have a mechanism in place to cleanse yourself mentally and begin each day *fresh, energetic, positive and on purpose.* Remember the human will is the strongest force and we are limiting it on account of the many mental injuries we hold dear.

16. What the greats have to say

WHEN I WAS a teenager, I used to pray to a poster of Sachin Tendulkar that I had atop my bed. I wanted him to bless me with his cover drives, straight hits, cuts and pulls. Needless to say, I was star struck. Celebrities and their tales are so inspiring that on a whim, we imbibe their value systems and imitate their personality traits.

With the kind of awe, attention and focus on them, their utterances tend to be accepted simply because of who they are. Growing up with starry eyes, this habit of mine suppressed my originality. Since my heroes were so wealthy and successful, I thought they had all the answers.

But the fact is, they are only human, no matter how the media projects them or no matter what they have accomplished. They suffer from the same issues the rest of us suffer. Fundamentally, their minds are of the same nature. They fail, feel confused, insecure, make wrong decisions, get jealous, suffer from arrogance and pray to the Gods for good fortune. They do all the things we do. There is no real reason to be intimidated by them at all.

Even in their thoughts and ideas about winning, losing, success, or failure, there is no unanimity. They have different views and some of them are just downright unscientific. But the common and consistent factor in people who have scaled great heights *is the inspired conviction and belief* in what they are doing. They stand firm by what they know works for them, and they insist on retaining their originality despite what the world says.

In this chapter, I have chosen some quotations by great sporting personalities of the present as well as of eras gone by. I want to bring out how different philosophies or thinking, no matter how contrasting, work equally well for different individuals.

Famous words

> Whoever said, 'It's not whether you win or lose that counts,' probably lost.
>
> – *Martina Navratilova*[90]

I am not privy to the context in which this statement was made. However, there are several thoughts that come to my mind when I read this quote.

Looking at it in isolation, it seems to be a belief suggesting that those who spend time and thoughts on philosophical approaches are probably the ones who have lost. Or put another way, those who are not obsessed with the idea of winning at all costs probably never win. And it's because they don't win, that they philosophise. This mirrors the attitude that the free-market culture promotes – zero tolerance for losing.

Today, winning is synonymous with being extremely competitive, forceful and aggressive. This is the quality that is coached into sportsmen: "You must be ruthless, you must have a killer instinct."

Why do today's youngsters react so violently, so aggressively? In earlier times, across sports, celebrations were sober, at least on the field. This entire attitudinal and behavioural shift can be attributed to multiple factors. Pressure has increased manifold today. This age of consumerism, media and massive corporate involvement in sport has added to the already existing pressures of national, personal and family honour. All these combine to form multiple millstones around one's neck.

The approach of, 'The means of achieving victory matters not, so long as victory is achieved,' will probably distance you from having a more humane approach to your sport. Under such conditions, chances of sportsmanship being compromised are rather high.

There are millions who watch and worship their sporting heroes, follow their every word and imitate their every move. These sportspeople are not just heroes but role models. I was a big fan of Lance Armstrong and it hurt me deeply when I learnt that he had cheated by taking performance-enhancing drugs. I admired him and hoped against hope that it wasn't true.

The emphasis placed these days on winning has corrupted the means. The sportsman spirit has taken a hit. The important question to ask is, does this really bring out the best in us? For a few minutes in the limelight, is it worth compromising every decent tradition of sportsmanship?

Perhaps the most infamous incident in cricket's history occurred during a one-day match between Australia and New Zealand (NZ) in1981. To tie the game, NZ needed a six off the last ball. At this point, Greg Chappell – Australia's then captain – instructed the bowler, his brother Trevor, to bowl underarm. Since the ball would roll along the ground, this ensured the six could not be hit. NZ duly lost.[91]

While Chappell's instruction was within the prevailing laws of the game, it was clearly against the spirit of fair play. New Zealand's Prime Minister at the time, Robert Muldoon, called it, "The most disgusting thing I can recall in the history of cricket. It was a true act of cowardice and I consider it appropriate that the Australian team were wearing yellow." The then Prime Minister of Australia, Malcolm Fraser, said the underarm ball was "Contrary to the traditions of the game."[92] Despite a glorious career, Greg Chappell is often remembered for the underarm ball, as opposed to some of his other cricketing feats.

Football has its own stories. The head butting of Italy's Marco Materazzi by the French great Zinedine Zidane in a World Cup game shocked millions. It brought Zidane's glorious and glittering career to a shameful end. It was later learned that Materazzi had sledged Zidane on a personal level. But why did Materazzi sledge him in the first place? It's almost certainly because he was subject to the unbelievable pressure of a World Cup game. All this is just a reflection of what the 'win at all costs' mentality can do to even the most seasoned of players.

On the other hand, India's cricketing great Gundappa Vishwanath is fondly remembered for calling back Bob Taylor after he was wrongly adjudged out in a Test match in 1980. I have played cricket in Karnataka for 14 years and I have yet to hear anybody say anything remotely critical about Mr Vishwanath. Humility and simplicity are endearing qualities and both exist in abundance in the man, ditto for legend Rahul Dravid.

In August 2011, India's captain Mahendra Singh Dhoni asked Ian Bell to return even after he was adjudged run out in a Test match against England. Praising Dhoni, Mr Vishwanath said, "For me, spirit of the game is of paramount importance rather than winning or losing a Test match. Obviously, as a captain you play hard to win a match, but there are times when it's your inner call that tells you what is right. I really appreciate Dhoni's decision to call Bell back."[93]

Sooner rather than later, everybody forgets victories and defeats no matter how dramatic. But shows of compassion that touch the hearts of the fans are always remembered. Men and women who revolutionised societies have used love, compassion and goodness as their tools or ideals, be it a Gandhi, Mother Teresa or Martin Luther King.

Now think of what could happen to a young, impressionable, sporting mind on hearing a remark like the one made by Martina Navratilova, one of the greatest tennis stars of all time. What she says is likely to be accepted as true without examination. Her quote is result oriented in nature, and we've discussed threadbare the potential psychological impact of such statements.

I will myself advocate a fanatical approach if it means that victory is a guaranteed outcome. But I have repeatedly found this to be false. Rather than Navratilova, I tend to agree with Jim Courier, a former world no.1 in men's tennis. He said:

> Sportsmanship for me, is when a guy walks off the court and you really can't tell whether he won or lost. When he carries himself with pride either way.
>
> - *Jim courier*[94]

Notice the contrast in the statements of the two former tennis greats. I can say with some confidence that Courier must know a thing or two about winning and competing at the highest level. Perhaps sportsmen like Courier have trained their mind to be indifferent to result, or possess a broader understanding of life and sport's place in it. When I first read Courier's quote, our very own Dhoni immediately sprung to mind. I find it hard to recall an instance where he has lost composure. He wears the same swagger, whether he gets out for naught or scores a century. The concept of bouncing back does not exist when you refuse to let outcome bounce you around.

Bharath Chipli, an IPL and Ranji player, once told me, "When a bowler gets me out, I especially make it a point to walk back confidently with my chest thrust out."

Normally, we're ecstatic and on top of the world when we win, and experience diametrically opposite emotions when we lose. From this innate condition emerges the fear of failure, because society has made defeat a grave and unimaginable thing that must be avoided at all costs.

What if the mind evolves to a degree that its thinking goes beyond victory and defeat?

WHAT IF?

What if mind realises the fact that happiness is not necessarily a product of victory? That happiness always exists in our hearts and we can access it anytime, unconditionally, in victory or defeat? Won't that knowledge itself make us a lot happier?

When a person understands this, he obviously operates from another gear. He wears a fearless attitude and the dread of failure loses its sting. Mostly, on account of false knowledge, the happiness in our hearts is triggered only when we perform well. That's why everyone is so desperate to succeed and that's also why we need to constantly boost our personality with victory to feel confident and happy. Our being is controlled by our ego, which cages the joy in our hearts and lets it out only under certain self-imposed conditions. But when we play from our hearts unconditionally, anything is possible.

When the mind does not depend on reward to feel fulfilled or content, such a mind approaches victory and defeat, success and failure, joy and sorrow, triumph and disaster, honour and dishonour, pleasure and pain, happiness and sadness, love and hate and other such seemingly dual mental states with a calmness of mind and temper.

This is what Lord Krishna tells Arjuna on the battlefield and describes such a person to be a "Sthitaprajna." Many centuries later the idea is still alive, and Jim Courier calls it true sportsmanship.

We find this age-old wisdom being embraced at Wimbledon too. Just above the player's entrance to the Centre Court, there is a line from Rudyard Kipling's poem "If":[95]

> If you can meet triumph and disaster and treat both these impostors just the same.

The poet uses the word 'If' because he understands this to be a lofty state of existence, not easily attainable. The human mind has fallen from its original blissful state of utter peace, calm and self-sufficiency.

The poet refers to 'triumph' and 'disaster' as both being imposters. He has seen that mankind is actually pursuing a joy that is permanent. But that permanency cannot be found in victory or in anything external. Deluded, our mind searches for it outside of itself, where it is never going to find it.

Kabir Das, a famous philosopher, spoke of how the musk deer stresses itself searching hither and yon for the source of the beautiful perfume that fills the air. It is unaware that the cause of the scent is a pouch hidden under its own tail.

Let's look at what Jesse Owens, a man who won four gold medals in the 1936 Summer Olympics in the sullen face of Adolf Hitler, said:

> In the end, it's extra effort that separates a winner from second place. But winning takes a lot more than that, too. It starts with complete command of the fundamentals. Then it takes desire, determination, discipline, and self-sacrifice. And finally, it takes a great deal of love, fairness and respect for your fellow man. Put all these together, and even if you don't win, how can you lose?[96]

The quotation stands out because of its sensitive nature. It further grows in significance when you learn that Mr Owens was an African-American athlete, the grandson of slaves growing up at a time when racism was rampant. After returning from the Olympic Games a champion, he was still looked at as a black man and not a hero. His family was refused accommodation at a number of New York hotels when they travelled there to welcome him home from Berlin.[97] He could have easily chosen to be bitter with the world, but he did not. Hence, his are the words of a true champion.

You can see how Mr Owens has placed before us an alternative approach to what constitutes winning and losing. When you commit yourself to the right values, you are already a winner no matter which way the result goes. The emphasis is entirely on the process and nothing else. In these conditions, the mind is made to understand that it is the journey that needs attention; it is really the only thing that is real. If you go back to Navratilova's quote, it can be strongly contested. For Mr Owens, a man of great stature and accomplishment, gives out the message in no uncertain terms that winning is a lot more than just achieving a certain outcome.

CONFUSION OF IDEAS

Rafael Nadal, after winning one of his many French Open titles, said that he is motivated by the fear of failing.[98] In the world of Hindi movies, superstar Shah Rukh Khan too has echoed the same message.[99] So you have two famous and highly decorated personalities saying what drives them is the fear of failing. This is opposite to what many of the world's sports psychologists, mental conditioning experts, sportsmen and women who are worth their salt will tell you.

Performance is the biggest casualty when one is enveloped in fear. Let's look at what Henry Ford, the American industrialist and the founder of The Ford Motor Company had to say about fear as a driving force: "One who fears failure limits his activities. Failure is the opportunity to more intelligently begin again.[100]

And here is a quote from Napoleon Bonaparte, the famous French military and political leader, "He who fears being conquered is sure of defeat."[101] The inventor Thomas Edison said, "I failed my way to success," after trying unsuccessfully not once or twice, but over 10,000 times before making the light bulb. When asked about his frustrations with several failed attempts he simply said, "I have not failed. I've just found 10,000 ways that won't work."[102]

Hence the saying, "Success is a result of good judgement, good judgement is a result of experience, and experience is often the result of bad judgment." Therefore to succeed, failure is inevitable. If you're failing, it's absolutely normal. The basketballer Michael Jordan said:

> I've missed more than 9000 shots in my career. I've lost almost 300 games. 26 times, I've been trusted to take the game winning shot and missed. I've failed over and over and over again in my life. And that is why I succeed.[103]

Such inspiring and authentic words are a result of intense experience and insight. We now have several perspectives on the same subject, all coming from very accomplished athletes who have played the sport at the highest level and in the most competitive environments.

NOBODY IS PERFECT

I think it is the right time for me to cite here what Mr Bill Gates, founder of Microsoft, has said in the past. He is the man responsible for taking desktop computing to the masses and is an authority and institution by himself. However, let's look at some of his bloopers:[104]

- There's nobody getting rich writing software that I know of.
- We will never make a 32-bit operating system.
- Spam will be a thing of the past in two years' time.

His company has certainly gotten rich writing software. Today we have products from his very company that run on 64 bit operating systems. And we still pray to God to do something about spam.

Even the greats get it wrong from time to time. They have to! Do not be stunned by their achievements and accept whatever they say blindly. Because from time to time, they say some awfully stupid things that can grossly mislead. After all, they are human beings and even when we call ourselves experts, the humanness in us makes mistakes.

Roger Bannister, the man who first ran the sub-four-minute mile, had this to say:

> Doctors and scientists said that breaking the four-minute mile was impossible, that one would die in the attempt. Thus, when I got up from the track after collapsing at the finish line, I figured I was dead.[105]

You must carve your own path, listen to everyone from the celebrity to the street hawker with an open unprejudiced mind, but above all, listen to that innocent voice in your heart. It's a lesson I took some time to learn. I would doubt myself and place great importance on what everyone else was saying. I lost the ability to listen to my inner voice. I had the talent, but the lack of conviction caused confusion.

A conflicting viewpoint about my technique or tips by a celebrated player or coach would throw my mind into disarray. These comments would go on playing endlessly in my mind, ultimately leading to dejection, hate and self-disapproval. How could I have belief when I was oscillating between various approaches without firmly giving any one a proper chance?

Moreover, the public's affections are fickle. I perform well and praise is heaped. I fail to perform and out come the brickbats. Even the great Sachin Tendulkar was booed off Wankhede Stadium, his home ground, after a string of low scores. Almost everyone, including so-called experts, called for his retirement. But did he quit? Of course not. It was in the same stadium, years later, that the Wankhede crowd gave him a grand and moving farewell, chanting 'Sachin! Sachin!'

Stand your ground during the hard times in full knowledge that, 'The darkest hour of the night is just before dawn.'

Through centuries, all the great men and women who have transformed societies and touched people's hearts have done so against immeasurable odds. They remained unmoved in the face of intensely charged opposition. And history remembers them as heroes and time vindicates their methods and stances.

Let me now give you the inside story on the making of a contemporary champion.

17. Never say die – The stories of Mumbai and Pravin Tambe

BEFORE LANDING in Mumbai to play cricket, I often heard stories from Mr Makarand Waingankar about the city and particularly its cricketers. Mr Waingankar is a wonderful storyteller and with his wealth of experience, has an anecdote for almost every situation. Being a consultant with the KSCA (Karnataka State Cricket Association), he would very often tell us that simply living in Mumbai builds character. I never fully understood what he meant at the time, and like many others, dismissed it as words from someone who is obviously biased towards Mumbai. How can living in a city build character, I thought. After experiencing eight seasons as a Mumbaikar, I have understood what he means.

The city's vibe

Every city has its own vibe. But if you've lived long enough in Mumbai and have connected with it, you will never want to live elsewhere. This possibly only a Mumbaikar will understand. What is so special about this city? What is the 'something' that endears it so much to its citizens? For when you look purely at the stats, they are not flattering.

The upshot of the city's popularity means its resources are strained. Housing is not cheap and a large proportion of Mumbai's residents live in slums that lack basic sanitation and hygiene. You can see the results of this on the streets and railway tracks. Competition for resources is fierce. Yet, there is a lot of love in Mumbai, and that is what fuels the great city. Love is the ultimate force that unlocks human potential.

But can merely living in a city unlock some of that potential? The question is, do the citizens make the city or the city its citizens? Who shapes whom? And this brings me to Mumbai's local train services.

The lifeline of Mumbai

The spirit of Mumbai is best understood through its local trains, especially during peak hours. When I first arrived in Mumbai, I lived in Airoli for 12 months during my first two seasons. An uncle of mine (President of the Coorg Association) convinced my parents to abandon all plans of having me live in Bandra and paying Rs 15,000 as rent. Instead, I lived at the Kodava Association building in a humble room with common toilets, paying Rs 500 as rent.

Airoli is quite far-off from several cricket grounds. I had to rely on the Mumbai local train services to get around for matches and practice sessions that were often in the 'town' area or in Bandra. I regularly needed to change three trains to reach my destination, wiping out over three hours each day.

I travelled by the general compartment. The hard pushing, nudging and prodding one has to endure in these locals was made doubly hard because of my rather large cricket kit bag. It was like two people entering the train. The kit bag was never popular with fellow commuters especially when the little space on the few overhead racks got full.

I often felt drowned and lost in the sheer multitude of humanity on the platforms and in the trains. The trains would arrive at the station like an overstuffed vada pav. No sane person would ever board a train already so packed. Considering myself sane, I waited patiently for the first few days, hoping the next local wouldn't be as full. But soon I realised my stupidity, as it only cost me more time and never made the journey less uncomfortable.

On entering a local train, you'll be instantly sucked into a battle with fellow commuters for a seat. With little or no space and people tightly pressed up against all sides of my body, I often felt violated. The only rule of the game – you snooze you lose.

Board a local during peak hours and you will understand why I say this. It takes a great deal of tact and awareness to know when exactly to enter, when to give an inch and be accommodative to another commuter, and when not to. The crowds are so fierce in entering and exiting that Darwin's theory, 'Survival of the fittest,' is proven true every second.

It was some time before I acquired the local knowledge necessary to feel relatively secure in what seemed like a hostile environment. For someone whose only previous exposure to public transport within a city was an auto rickshaw, it took me a while to blend in.

Nonetheless, all this was an education that built both character and strength. The whole process made me street-smart. No kidding! Above all, I learnt about total surrender. I say surrender because the Mumbai local continues to operate in the face of almost insurmountable odds. Obviously, there must be some kind of providence involved!

Mumbai's compassion and inclusiveness

As competitive as people are, I also noticed the softer side of this city. Notwithstanding the discomforts of a crammed, sweaty, sticky compartment, it's an unspoken rule that you're expected to stick out your hand and help pull in a person seeking to come on board. Is it instinct, practice, or an inherited natural compassion? Don't ask, it's just what the Mumbaikar in a local will do and it's no big deal to him or her.

I once saw in Vashi station an old lady lose hold of her young grandson in the rush while getting off the train. The child got off in time but the old lady could not, as she was overwhelmed by the rush of people seeking to get inside. Neither the lady nor her grandson had a mobile phone. I took the child to the stationmaster, who promised to make the necessary announcements and arrangements. Mercifully, I heard from an attendant the next day that the little boy had been reunited with his grandmother.

The Mumbai local is simultaneously a melting pot and meeting point. White collar or blue collar, student or hawker – all their identities dissolve as they become one when they board a local. Regardless of the God they venerate, they become nothing more than a bunch of individuals struggling in identical conditions in a journey together.

Over time, travelling in the Mumbai local subtly instils compassion. I say compassion because *it is a train that has a big heart*, whose doors are forever open and ready to accommodate one more, no matter how full. The fact that Mumbaikars often praise their train service so much is proof enough that they have wholeheartedly come to accept the inclusive nature of their city and its transport lifeline. The more time I spent there, the more I felt the city's character gradually growing into me too.

I have seen this character of the Mumbai local imbibed in the cricketers, whom I played alongside for eight seasons.

The cricketing culture

The city has a long-standing tradition of rolling out world-class cricketers. Purely in terms of talent, I feel my home state Karnataka is better off but when it comes to application, the Mumbaikars are years ahead. I attribute this to the way life is conducted, and also to the strong cricketing culture that is unique to the city.

The local leagues are treated with great respect. All top players participate in the matches and this maintains a high standard of play. As recently as a year ago, a former Test player played a game in a maidan (ground) for his club. So these big guns are not only aware but also nurture the talent coming through the ranks.

In comparison to Karnataka, Mumbai has twice as many local tournaments. There are even tournaments running parallel to the Ranji Trophy season. This places a continual and healthy competitive pressure on those in the Ranji squad, as every good performance in these tournaments is treated seriously. Selectors seem relatively open to pick anybody.

Another obvious advantage of multiple tournaments is multiple opportunities. The entire cricket population is kept engaged in matches, giving everyone a chance to recover from injuries or bad form, and make comebacks.

The personality of players

I had to leave Airoli at 6am to reach the ground in Churchgate or CST station by 8am. After travelling so much, one feels intensely determined to make the most of the afforded opportunity. Almost every player travels long distances and the whole process serves up a way of life that makes you hardened. If it's not love for the game that's driving you, there will be no sense in undertaking such hardships.

It's rare to see a player with a laid back approach on the field. Despite the intensity, I have rarely been sledged while playing in Mumbai. The players are approachable, friendly and helpful. The best part is their attitude which is, "It's no big deal." But then again if you upset them, you've had it.

Mumbai instils in them values that squeeze out their potential, as they treat every opportunity that comes their way with the sanctity it deserves. All this and more contributes to the fact that Mumbai has won the Ranji Trophy no less than 40 times.

A tribute

Mumbai looks me in the face as if to say:

> I don't care that you judge me. You may say I am polluted, overcrowded, dusty, crude and suffocating. Though filled with shanties that are ugly and unhygienic, you miraculously find in them more

smiling faces than you ever will in some of the more 'modernised' parts that you frequent. Can you rationalise that?

I am not saying for a moment that I am easy to understand, but let me explain myself.

I am part rural and part urban and have for the longest time been called the 'city of dreams.' I am diverse and attract all to me. People like you, from every corner of the country, of different cultures, cuisines, costumes, character and goals approach me in search of expansion. The sheer numbers and dreams I have to satisfy are a lot more than I can handle, and hence I don't sleep, I am ever at the wheel. For, everyone who lands on my shores deserves a fighting chance.

Though I satisfy most, there are some whose expectations I may not meet, yet I take care that all are nourished.

Despite all my apparent imperfections, my inhabitants are ever active, free of sloth and always looking to break boundaries and move beyond their limitations. They don't wait for the day when everything is ideal; they strive to make the most of what they have. This is my soul, the Mumbai soul.

Metaphors have been used to describe my resilience. I have been through many ups and downs, innumerable attempts have been made to break me and yet not only do I survive, I thrive. I may be hard to understand, but what can I say, I am mysterious and refuse definition.

I am Mumbai, the city of the great mother, Mumba.

This is my romantic perception of a city that has provided my cricketing soul salvation.

The making of a champion – Pravin Tambe

Champions don't become champions in the ring – they are merely recognised there.

– Unknown

At age 41, Pravin Tambe made his debut for both Mumbai and Rajasthan Royals (RR). He entered the public imagination after receiving the Golden Ball (for being the highest wicket-taker) in the 2013 Champions League. Prior to his debut in IPL, he had not played in a single match at the first class level. Such a thing is unheard of in India, where the Ranji Trophy or first class tag is essential for a place in any major team.

Mr Kuruvilla says this of Tambe: "Pravin is someone with the enthusiasm and energy of an 18 year old, combined with the maturity of a 40 year old." Tambe embodies the spirit of Mumbai. He is humble, caring, resilient, and a complete family man. He has an unquestionable air of self-assurance.

For eight seasons, Pravin was my captain at DYPSA. His story is unique and worthy of our attention because it is path breaking. It's important to keep in mind that he never intentionally attempted to create a new path, defy the system or set a new benchmark. It all happened naturally and for that reason, he is the epitome for what playing out of pure unadulterated love for the game can bring you.

Given the nature of his cricketing journey, I decided to interview him for this book. With his permission, I have reproduced excerpts from a recorded conversation I had with him. Prashant Bhoir, a longtime friend and contemporary of Tambe's was also present. Bhoir is himself an ex-Maharashtra Ranji player and a current DY-ite.

Conversation with Pravin Tambe: The IPL Experience

(The interview has been transcribed with only minor edits. At the time of the interview Tambe had not the slightest idea of the overall message of this book)

Tambe began by describing his IPL experience. Initially, he spent most of his time warming the benches. For a handful of games that season, his captain Rahul Dravid had him as part of the 12, but he never made the playing 11. Finally, when Tambe's urge to play a game grew overwhelmingly strong, he decided to speak up.

He said to his captain, "Rahul bhai, I'm a team man. But keep one thing in mind, I am very much confident about myself; if I play in any match I can perform, I have got the confidence. I am not saying I am unhappy with the team you are picking for tomorrow, but just be open to playing me."

Dravid replied, "Yes, I know Pravin, I know you."

Tambe told me, "Then I finally got my opportunity, not because I spoke to him but only because it was the right cricketing decision."

After a few games in IPL 2013, Tambe injured his finger and could not make much of an impact for the rest of the tournament. He got his next chance in the Champions League that followed the IPL. He made that tournament his own, with a much-celebrated four-wicket haul against the Highveld Lions.

Me: **How did those four wickets happen?**
Tambe: *Just with good practice, encouragement from the seniors especially James Faulkner and Brad Hodge. If you are comfortable bowling against Brad Hodge and Shane Watson yaar you will get that confidence.*

Me: **Normally the shift in atmosphere from maidans to packed stadiums impact a player's mind. Did the shift affect you?**
Tambe: *No, not at all. Honestly, I didn't feel anything; I did not feel like I am playing this level or that level. When I was on the ground, I never felt in any single over that I am under any pressure or I have got any burden.*

Me: **Why do you think you didn't feel nervous?**
Tambe: *I honestly don't know why. But maybe the atmosphere in the team was like that and nobody was under pressure. All were encouraging to go express yourself and do whatever you were doing for so many years, that was Rahul bhai's advice. Just go express yourself, think that you are playing in your club or company match and just perform. That's the thing you want ya from your captain, confidence.*

Me: **I am very curious to know how the entire IPL thing happened. You played so many years in the Mumbai leagues, and did you at any stage expect IPL to happen?**
Tambe: *No, never. I never expected actually the Mumbai call also. I was first picked for the Vijay Hazare knockout (first class) tournament at age 41, for the first time ever, just before IPL.*

Me: **On the basis of which performance did you get the call from Mumbai?**
Tambe: *On the basis of my local performance, the All-India D Y Patil T20 tournament, you know better na you were playing in DY T20.*

***Me:* I want to understand the means through which it all happened. I was told that your resume was sent to a few states, but was rejected each time because of your age. What do you think changed here in Mumbai? Who was particularly impressed with you, impressed enough to say, ok, let's go against all rules and pick this 41 year old?**
Tambe: *That I also want to know (smiling), who was that person who picked me. I don't know for sure. I must mention here Mr Abey Kuruvilla (our Sports Director) along with Zubin Barucha and Monty Desai from RR who were of great help, and the ones who really know what I am about.*

(I'm taking a detour at this stage to talk about how ossified ideas about age and other stereotypes act as huge barriers in the minds of many selectors, administrators, and scouts. I'll resume the conversation with Tambe after that.)

THE AGE FACTOR

Age is no barrier, it's a limitation you put on your mind.[106]

– Jackie Joyner Kersee, winner of several Olympic medals

"Am I too old, have I missed the bus?" This was the thought that too often plagued my mind and that of my contemporaries. We felt very guilty to be playing cricket seriously once we passed age 24. 'Make it in age-group cricket or just chuck your dreams,' was the attitude.

It is the mind that is the problem, and its faulty notions often become institutionalised. In Mumbai, they don't seem to worry too much about age. They seem to pick you if you perform consistently. Mr Kuruvilla told me, "Here, if you are in good form we will pick you, age does not bother us." Coming from an ex-Mumbai selector, it was refreshing to hear.

In some ways, Sachin Tendulkar's Mumbai debut at age 15 and India debut at age 16 caused problems for almost everyone else. Since he broke into the highest level so early, the nation got a new benchmark age for making it big. State associations across the country began looking only for very young prodigies. I asked Mr Irfan Sait, who runs a cricket academy in Bengaluru, about why children have to start entering camps at age seven or eight and sometimes even younger, and be subjected to serious coaching.

"Work backwards," he said. "It stands to reason that if you expect a child to play Ranji Trophy by age 18, he will have to start training at a much younger age."

As a result, the pressure is on us to have our career paths track the big names. If that fails to happen, we become agitated and start to take on feelings of lack and lose our sense of proportion. False birth certificates have become a huge racket as a result.

Today, every association expects a cricketer to be playing at the first class level by age 22 at the very latest. Since players are from different backgrounds, not everyone matures or acquires skills at the same pace. It is foolhardy to make a once-in-a-generation genius like Tendulkar the gold standard against which everyone else is measured. Far from stemming this trend, the custodians of the game only encourage it.

How many Indian or even international cricketers have debuted for their countries at age 16 after Tendulkar? Not a single one. He is called a genius because he is special, one of a kind, so also Tiger Woods and Roger Federer. While all these super achievers play different sports, they share the following traits:

- They are endowed with greater natural ability than most others.
- They begin intense practice at a very young age.
- They have good mentors and a support system that gives them expert guidance and instils good values.
- They arrive at methods, insights and maturity about the game sooner than most do.

It's rare for all these factors to come together in one person, and when they do, we say he is endowed with a 'super-natural' ability. Many of us have read Malcolm Gladwell's argument that 10,000 hours of work is necessary for one to become a genius.[107]

The worst thing parents and sporting bodies can do is to expect the same kind of success from their kids and push them too hard. They will end up hurting them. It's like trying to pass a powerful jolt of electricity through a low-capacity light bulb. The bulb will get stressed and burst, and it wouldn't be the bulb's fault.

Everyone Deserves One More Chance

Ultimately, it's better to allow something to grow in its own time and oversee it, than force it to grow faster and destroy it in the process. For instance, Mike Hussey has had an international cricket career as good as any. He debuted for Australia at age 30. Dirk Nannes made his first class debut at age 29 and played for Australia 2-3 years later. Regarding Pravin

Tambe, Mr Kuruvilla says, "Pravin has been bowling his best in the last 4 to 5 years."

The irony in India is that on one hand we have Sachin Tendulkar, who was living his dream at 16, and on the other, we have Tambe's career finding wings at a time when most retire. Both selections happened in Mumbai, reflecting the open-mindedness and fearlessness of the selectors. Thanks to them, it is possible for a player between the ages of 16 and 42 to be picked, and even this 'rule' can be broken.

Returning to the conversation with Pravin Tambe: On motives

Tambe: *One thing for sure yaar now, at least in Mumbai cricket no one will say that, "Oh I have not got selected for U-19, my career is gone or I have not got selected for U-25 my career is gone." I think everyone will keep working now.*

Me: **At such a late age what motivates you to continue playing, is it for name and fame?**

Tambe: *Just love for the game, and I want to keep that. I don't want to miss a single game. In IPL people used to ask me, "Why you want to play for Mumbai and all ya at this age." If you ask me, if I am fit and fine I want to play this game, each and every game.*

Me: **So this love you have for the game, has this attitude been there right through your career?**

Tambe: *Yes, right through! I used to play football earlier, but once I shifted over to cricket, yes (pauses). My mind goes back to when I got married in October 1998, four months before that I fractured my leg in an accident, while trying to catch a train. My leg was in a plaster. And my Australia tour was due – the Common Wealth Bank emerging player tour.*

It was a 15-day camp and I was looking forward to it. So what I did was take off my plaster in 12 days, honestly, so I could prove my fitness in a tournament before that tour! Unfortunately, they did not pick me. I wanted to go play because I am a leg spinner and I heard there might be Shane Warne who could give you tips. And after I got man of the series, I expected that I might go to Australia now, but my manager said, "No, no you are still injured." He gave me some exercise and I showed him that I can do it, but he still did not take me. I wanted to go to Australia to play cricket only, nothing else. That was my love.

(At this stage, Tambe's friend Prashant Bhoir enters the conversation.)
***Bhoir:* You would sometimes say that you weren't getting the opportunities due to you. Were you frustrated then?**
Tambe: *I was also telling everyone that I am not disappointed. I like this game and I will keep playing the game. You never know what is going to happen tomorrow you know. That's what I am doing actually. Every single game I love to play. As long as I am playing, I am happy. However, at one point, I thought my career will be gone because of injuries. I have had many injuries, but somehow my body always recovered.*

***Me:* You have used the word 'love' in every instance to describe your feeling for the game as opposed to 'passion.' Any specific reason for that?**
Tambe: *I think both actually, passion also and love also for this game should be in every cricketer.*

Bhoir: *I think whatever helps you enjoy the game and takes away the pressure. Tambe used to play everywhere, wherever there is a match he used to play. Now if you tell me go play any match, I will say no yaar, but if you tell him there is some random match here or there, even in the evening after a day's game he will go, even at 40, I don't know why.*

Tambe: *Because I love this game yaar, I want to play, I am not knowing whether we are going to win or lose, but I just want to go and play cricket.*

Facing competition

***Me:* So all through your 30s did you ever give up saying, "Ok, I will probably never play Ranji Trophy"?**
Tambe: *See, first thing is I was never thinking about Ranji Trophy. I was only thinking about how I am going to continue playing cricket.*

***Me:* Ok, but looking at the other bowlers around, did you at some point think, "How I bowl, and yet these other players are getting selected instead of me," and feel troubled?**
Tambe: *I think you have played with me for six or seven years and honestly, you can ask anybody in our team, they will tell you I always praised those who made the Ranji Trophy squad. I would always tell them well done and keep working hard. I was enjoying playing my cricket and no one stopped me from*

playing cricket yaar. That was enough for me. So why should I think which level I am going to play or pull anyone down. I wanted to play this game. That's all.

***Me:* You told me that Shilpa Shetty (RR team owner) called you and said, "Most people want to take a picture with me but I want to take a picture with you." Do you think all this extra attention you're getting after IPL will change your motives?**

***Tambe:** I am here because of cricket. I play cricket with love and am not thinking about anything right now and I don't think I will in the future also. And I never think about fame and all that you said before. Nothing can change my love for cricket yaar.*

***Me:* I would often think, "I never got a hundred" or "I never got picked" or "That guy got picked and is getting all the attention and I'm not......"**

(Tambe interjects vehemently at this point.)

***Tambe:** But that is not love for the game na yaar, and that needs to be emphasised and understood. If you are loving this game why do you want to think about what is going to happen? Arre Ashwath, I used to play tennis ball cricket first and underarm also, for 13 or 14 years. I was a professional cricketer in tennis ball first, not just overarm but underarm also, it's very popular in Mumbai. I always played. It was never about money or anything.*

(I'm taking another detour here to look a little deeper into why I am stressing so much on motive and intention. When we reconnect with Tambe, we will discuss his family, financial situation and more.)

Love moves the world, why not cricket?

I said at the start that love unlocks human potential; Tambe is a fitting example of love being the best driving force that will inevitably bring you the rewards. Love for craft and success are not mutually exclusive but complementary.

When Steve Jobs was asked how he felt when Apple's earnings crossed that of Microsoft's, he replied, "Well, that's not the reason why we turn up for work every day. We turn up because we love what we do."[108] This is the kind of unconditional love for craft that leads you to the summit and keeps you there for long years.

Another splendid example is that of the chairman of the DYPSA group, Mr Vijay Patil. His love for sports, particularly cricket, is tremendous. It's the same love that has driven him to build what is arguably one of the best stadiums in the world. Much like the Taj Mahal, it stands as a symbol of love – of one man's love for sports. He could have done a million other things with the money for a healthier ROI (Return on Investment), but funny are the ways of love. Mr Patil has made D Y Patil and Navi Mumbai a centre for cricket in Mumbai and India. Like me, many cricketers, sportsmen and fitness enthusiasts are beneficiaries of the great facilities.

One morning when in Nerul, Mr Patil asked me to meet him in his office at 7:30am. He wanted to discuss his management college venture and enquired if my software company could handle the online side of things. Once we finished with that, the conversation inevitably shifted to cricket.

He spoke about how local politicians were getting worried that he may enter politics, after his popularity had risen following the stadium's completion. He said to me, "I know I will do well if I enter politics, but I am not interested. I want to do what I love doing. At the time of building this stadium, there was no IPL and people thought I was crazy. Most people were worried as to how I would recover the funds. But I wanted a state-of-the-art facility for sports and the risk had to be taken. We went ahead, then the IPL happened and opportunities began to flow."

The conversation with Mr Patil reinforced two points for me:

- When you desire to do something from your heart, you must be brave enough to take a stand, regardless of whether it seems logical or not. When you do, you find circumstances aligning themselves in time to show you the way.
- Love is the greatest driving force.

Most of us who play sport professionally love the game wholeheartedly, but have almost forgotten how to play out of love. With time, various pressures have clouded our minds and replaced our original motives. We must therefore be eternally vigilant. So long as one's motives are driven by lust for reward, wealth, power or even revenge, one's mind remains agitated.

Importance of Dispassion

The word 'passion' is way too overrated and overused. It is more harmful than useful, and in the following few paragraphs I'll share my thoughts on why I say this.

There is a difference that exists between love and passion. Minds driven by love, and minds driven by passion, differ in quality. By definition, passion means a 'barely controllable emotion.' Passion is probably the cruder form of love. If passion ever had an ambition it would be to become love someday. There is a certain compulsion, desperation and rowdiness in passion that is absent in love.

Love fears nothing, it embraces all outcomes. It is fearless because it cannot be subject to condition, as Tambe's career proves. Love gets demoted to passion when the poisons of possessiveness, obsession, and expectation creep in.

In highly toxic or pressurised environments, this can easily happen. We have heard of crimes of passion, where passion turns violent and all reasoning capacities of the mind are lost. Hence, cultivating dispassion or indifference to outcome is showing true love for your craft. Otherwise joy can quickly turn to sorrow and pleasure to pain.

To promote obsession in the name of passion is not healthy or advisable. Cultivate love for craft instead. But if you insist on being passionate, be so about the journey, and utterly dispassionate about the result.

This does not mean negativity or insensitivity. When understood from a spiritual perspective, dispassion is indeed very positive. It is only when one knows that he has nothing to lose or hold on to, that one can be utterly free from the fear of failure. Fearlessness and love go hand in hand because both are free of conditions and boundaries.

(I now return to the conversation with Tambe.)

Off the field challenges

***Me:* Your main source of income is cricket and you got a big break only at 41. Did the financial aspect ever bother you?**

Tambe: *When I was in England in 2004 with my wife and child, I came to know all cricketers at my then employer had lost their jobs, including myself, so I was worried.*

***Me:* How did you handle that?**

Tambe: *I took it sportingly. I said I am still playing cricket so I will get a job somewhere in India. I gave a call to a company in Mumbai that hires cricketers. There the boss said, "You don't worry, you come here and we will give you a job." But when I came to India and went to them, they did not give me a job. Then I*

gave interviews with two to three companies but nothing happened. Finally one company offered me only Rs 1,600. Can you believe that, in 2004, 1,600 Indian rupees as monthly salary including my travel. I was about 32 then.
I told them I was married with a child, and have work experience for 10 years. They said, "You don't have relevant experience. But we want you to play cricket for us and we will give you job, and within six months you will get a pay rise." When I asked how much they said it will come to Rs 2,500. I wanted a job and so I said, "Yes." For a month, I was working from 9am – 6pm. One day I had a game on the weekend for Shivaji Park Gymkhana, and they were not allowing me to play that game.

They said, "No, you have to do overtime. You have not learned your job yet, that's why you should stay back." That's when I just took my bag and quit the job. I said I want to play cricket and I went for that game because it was an important match for us. I never thought about my family that time, I wanted to play cricket, so I took my bag and left. We won that game, and afterwards I started thinking about losing my job and what next and all that. I was worried.

***Me:* Did that affect your performance on the field?**
Tambe: *When I went on the field it never affected. After a few weeks I got a call from Mr Abey Kuruvilla. He asked, "Are you interested in playing for DY Patil?" I said, "Very much," but I added, "I want a job first and then cricket," for the first time in my life. Abey said, "You will play cricket and get a job both," and so in 2005 I joined DY Patil.*

***Me:* How did you manage with that kind of money?**
Tambe: *The money was not much, but we could manage, because we never had a craving for luxurious things. In fact, after playing IPL the first year was when I got myself a trouser for Rs 2,500. I had never bought that costly a trouser previously in my life.*

***Me:* Did playing in England for six months a year help?**
Tambe: *Some monetary benefits I was getting, but I had not played first class level, so I was an amateur cricketer and they don't pay amateur cricketers. It is a rule, so I was getting gifts from the families and friends over there, and that really helped me.*

Bhoir: *His wife has a big influence on him.*

Tambe: *Obviously yaar, family has a role yaar in all this. Because before marriage my parents never told me, "Why you are staying out of the house at night and playing, you have to do something for your life, for your future." And after marriage, if your partner keeps arguing with you that you are always away and never give the family time, it is very difficult. That's why I give credit to my wife, in these 14 years she never told me, "Stop playing cricket and look after family." Why? Because she knew that I am playing cricket but looking after family also, and she helps me a lot you know, because I hardly give time to my children.*
I must also thank my brother Prashant Tambe, he would encourage me saying, "Aap toh kuch bada hi karega" (you will definitely do something big).

HIS GOD AND HIS MIND

***Me:* Your journey has been unique; do you do anything to look after your mind, like prayer, meditation or belief in God?**
Tambe: *I believe in God, I really do. We all are Shirdi Sai Baba's bhakts. But I also worship other forms. I owe my success to everyone actually. Not only God. Because I felt in Champions League I had some extra energy with me. At no stage did I feel down or tired, honestly. I had an extra energy, I don't know why. So obviously it must also be the good wishes and prayers of my family and friends. I could feel that.*

***Me:* Normally how is your prayer?**
Tambe: *What do I ask from God? Just give your blessing to me, rest I will do. Just be with me every time. And whenever I go on the field I think all prayers are with me, I feel my prayer to God is answered and He is with me. Even if I win the game or lose the game I always think that He is with me. That's what helps me. I am not extreme, but I believe in God and that belief gives me strength and peace of mind, both.*

Bhoir: *We do visualisation, mental toughness exercises, read books and all, you don't, but you're still so mentally tough. How is that?*

Tambe: *I train my mind and my mind in turn trains my body. See, if you have to run for half an hour, my body won't agree for half an hour, but I will tell my body, "Listen you have to run for half an hour." Even if my body is tired, my mind doesn't give in. I talk to myself and say "Come on, just five more minutes." Same thing I apply for everything in life.*

Me: **Thanks a lot Pravin, I have taken a lot of your time, and I think it is clear now that you fully deserve your success and the readers, particularly the young lot, would have also learnt a lot from this interaction.**

Tambe: *You're welcome yaar, anytime.*

CHICKEN OR THE EGG?

Is it only performance that can bring confidence, happiness and success or should you be happy and confident first for success to follow in lockstep?

My point is that Tambe was always a great bowler who showed tremendous character. All through the seven years that I played with him, he never once spoke to me about the technical and tactical aspects of the game. He bowled, batted and captained from his heart and his heart taught him well enough. Also, despite being a hard working leg-spinner who often got hit for runs, I have never seen him swear or fight with any of the opposition players.

I remember telling my teammates in Jawahars (my former club in Bengaluru) that there is a brilliant leg spinner in Mumbai who is good enough to play for India, but has sadly not even played Ranji Trophy. Since Tambe was not known then, no one cared to listen. I had even spoken a lot about him to my close friend Udit Patel (Karnataka Ranji player), who reserved judgement assuming I was exaggerating. Some time later Udit himself joined the DY Patil side and played under Tambe's captaincy; he was astonished that a player of such calibre had not played even first class cricket.

I want to cite a couple of instances of my own experience playing with this 'peaceful warrior' that speaks volumes of his continuous faith in the 'anything is possible' attitude in life.

TWO STANDOUT EXPERIENCES WITH TAMBE

The first instance occurred in the last session of the final day of a match. Our opponents had obtained the first innings lead and were over 150 runs ahead with nine wickets in hand, with only an hour and a half of play left. The wicket was only getting better and better for batting. Following the tea break, most expected to play another 15 or 20 minutes before the match was called off.

In the customary huddle before taking the field our captain Tambe told us, "Chalo boys, 20 minutes mein hum teen teen hat-trick nikalke wapas run marenge." ("Come on boys, in 20 minutes let's take 3 hat-tricks and hit the runs.") He was serious!

One of my team-mates retorted, "Kya Pravin bhai teen teen hat-trick kaise?" ("How are three hat-tricks possible?"). Everyone burst out laughing almost to Tambe's surprise. Finally he laughed too. But such was his attitude. Whatever the situation, his approach remained the same.

The second incident is one where this attitude bore fruit. It was the year that saw DY Patil win the 'A' division Times Shield for the very first time in the club's history. In the semi-finals that season, we were chasing a mammoth target of 432. Our last wicket batsmen, Tambe and Kshemal, were at the crease with a little over 140 runs to get for victory. Most in the team had given up hope.

Long story short, the pair chased down the target in an amazing display of grit and stroke-play. In the process they achieved what most will call the impossible. It was extremely exciting and I was counting down the runs with a pen and sheet of paper. With two runs to go, Tambe swung wildly at a ball. It flew off the edge of his bat and through the hands of 2nd slip for a boundary. We danced with joy and crowded our heroes. We celebrated yet another sterling performance by our captain, but this time, with his bat.

Pointers on the Tambe Way

- He never played to 'make it big' in the game or to become a star, he played for the sake of playing, for the joy of it.
- He enjoyed the bonus of not having to deal with thoughts of expectation, or deal with feelings of jealousy that trouble so many.
- It is the purity of his intention that allowed him to bounce back quickly from setbacks. He could easily accept outcomes and move on in life.
- He is so conditioned by love for cricket that it made him extraordinarily positive and believe that anything is possible.
- It made the perseverance (20 years of *tapas* as our ancient wisdom calls it) possible and the journey enjoyable. *Because it is in perseverance that character is transformed.*
- His clarity and conviction made other people's opinions irrelevant.

- His rather simple and not so demanding lifestyle and cooperative family permitted him to pursue cricket.
- Love managed all the factors so intelligently for him. The only battle he fought was to stay fit, so he could continue playing the game. His approach might sound idealistic for some of you. But he has proved that there's place for such idealism. Even if it's at the age of 41.

18. Once upon a time in India

IN CHAPTER TWO, we saw the conditions that emerge in a society in which wealth and fame are linked to status. These ideas are so ingrained that I doubt whether the current generation can even fathom a different idea of society. Therefore, I wanted to explore if there was ever a time in history when:

- Status was not linked to wealth and fame.
- Simplicity and sacrifice were celebrated over vanity.
- Politicians, kings and kingmakers (teachers) were of noble intent.
- Overall education was man-making and not merely money-making.

Basically, I wanted to know if there ever was a system of education that made a person *independent of external gratification*, and not dependent on it. If there was indeed such an India, how did it function?

When I did some digging, I found sufficient evidence that pointed to the existence of such an India. In particular, the writings of two visitors to India stand out. The first is the work of Hieun Tsang, a 6th century Chinese scholar. The second is the *Indica* or account of India by Megasthenes, a Greek ambassador in the court of Chandragupta Maurya.

I was surprised and elated to learn that I belonged to a country that was once a global super-power both materially and *spiritually*. Yes, that's right! While India may seem far away from super-power status today, pay heed to the perspective offered by Shashi Tharoor, noted author and politician: "India is not, as people keep calling it, an underdeveloped country, but rather, in the context of its history and cultural heritage, a highly developed one in an advanced state of decay."[109]

Perhaps by going back in time, we may find a way forward.

A THROWBACK IN TIME

"Satyamev Jayate" – Truth Alone Triumphs. An English judge in India during the 19th century, William Sleeman, wrote in his book *Journey through Oudh*, "I have had before me hundreds of cases in which a man's property, liberty or life depended on his telling a lie and he has refused to tell it."[110]

Can we imagine such a thing today? But the larger question is, what were the conditions that made such a commitment to truth possible?

It's amply clear that the social order as originally devised by our ancients was meant to give power to the people of 'truth.' In other words, to give those individuals with experiential understanding of *'That'* (in the spiritual sense) the highest status in society. For a long time there existed a society that admired and respected men and women who lived a life of simplicity and sacrifice. The importance of being truthful first, beyond all other considerations is seen even as recently as the life of Mahatma Gandhi.

The occupation of people depended entirely on their own psychological inclinations, natural capacities and talents. Individuals were supposed to use their talents to fulfil particular roles required in society. As originally planned, the social order was born out of truths of human nature and developed for the best possible evolution of the human body, mind and soul. Work was to be treated as an instrument to evolve the mind, by renouncing the fruits of action.

The other noteworthy feature of the social system in its truest sense was that *wealth and status were de-linked.* A person with spiritual wealth was revered the most and used that knowledge to guide society. Kings, traders, warriors and farmers, all sought the advice of the wise.

To sum up, when wealth and status were delinked, the results were:

- A man's activity depended on talent – there was merit and skill in society.
- There was no grave identity crisis – society was designed to bring out spiritual identities.
- Simplicity was celebrity – simplicity was a way of life as thought processes were not linked to name and fame.
- Conduct and virtue were at the heart – society was process oriented because the means mattered as much as the goal.

Politics, governance and education

What was India like when it was the most prosperous nation on earth? What were the political ideas that powered our leaders? What values did they promote? What role did religion play? What qualities did the average Indian of the time possess and how did it translate in society?

For these questions, we have the reliable observations of Megasthenes and Hiuen Tsang. Their writings coincide with two periods in Indian history that are marked out for praise by historians. These are the glory periods of the Maurya empire (320-185 BC) and the Gupta eras (320-550AD). The Gupta eras are often referred to as the 'Golden age of India.'

The first names of the founding members of both dynasties were Chandragupta. Beyond their names, these two emperors shared other more important and noteworthy similarities, which we shall soon find out.

Mauryan era

Chandragupta Maurya is considered the first unifier of India and credited for making India a leading world power. The Mauryan flag flew over an area of well over three million sq km. It was one of the world's biggest kingdoms and the largest ever in the Asian subcontinent. India, parts of Afghanistan, Bangladesh, Pakistan and other surrounding areas were part of its territory.

Under the Maurya rulers, agriculture, trade and economic activities flourished, helped along by competent systems of finance, administration, and the military. Megasthenes observed that Indians "Love finery and ornament. Their robes are worked in gold and ornamented with precious stones, and they wear also flowered garments made of the finest muslin.[111]

R C Majumdar, also known as 'The dean of Indian historians,' writes in his book *Ancient India:*

> Both in central government as well as in the provinces, the administration was carried on by a number of departments, each under a superintendent, aided by a host of ministerial officers. There was a highly organised bureaucracy that efficiently managed the affairs of the vast empire. The different parts of the empire were connected by high roads, one of them traversing the whole breadth of India from the Sindu to the mouth of the Ganga. Irrigation works were undertaken even in such distant parts of the empire as the Kathiawar Peninsula, and, on the whole the efficiency of the government was combined with peace, prosperity and contentment of the people.[112]

The population of the empire has been estimated to be about 50-60 million, yet social harmony was maintained. The said period is referred to as the classical period of Indian history, during which time India was estimated to have the world's largest economy. It was undoubtedly a vast, peaceful, culturally rich and prosperous empire.

What drove this prosperity? For starters, let's take a peek into the life of the leader, and maybe we can understand this question better.

The leader – Chandragupta Maurya

Accounts of Chandragupta Maurya's early childhood are sketchy and various versions exist. Some say he was an offspring of the Nanda dynasty whose reign he later ended. Others say he was orphaned and raised in a humble home before being taken away by a man who saw a spark in him. This man picked up the boy from obscurity, as it were, and educated him in matters of warfare and governance, making a king out of him. The man was none other than Chanakya or Kautilya, the famous author of the Arthashastras and often referred to as 'King Maker.' Let us look at the environment that conditioned the boy under the patronage and guidance of his mentor par excellence.

Chandragupta was educated at Takshashila or Takshila (Taxila), the world's first university. The university had over 10,000 students, including many from places as distant as Greece, Arabia, China and Babylonia. A wide range of courses was taught including medicine, mathematics, law, art, archery, astronomy and philosophy.

Kautilya was no ordinary person. He mentored both Chandragupta Maurya and his son Bindusara (father of the Great Ashoka) and built their personalities on principles necessary to run their kingdoms effectively. The Arthashastras, comprising over 6,000 verses, are a marvel. They have a wealth of insight on management, economics, administration, politics, defence, strategy and a host of other subjects.

People often characterise Kautilya as cunning and shrewd, but when you read his thoughts, you soon understand the notion had to be a myth. A book called *Corporate Chanakaya* by Radhakrishnan Pillai outlines how these principles can be applied in the 21st century workplace. Here are a few lines from that book:

> As Chanakya himself says about the benefits of the Arthashastras – "This science (of Arthashastra) brings into being and preserves

> spiritual good, material wellbeing and pleasures, and destroys spiritual evil, material loss and hatred.[113]

> In the very first chapter of 'Arthashastra,' titled 'The topic of training,' he outlines the importance of a spiritual foundation. Ethics and morals were top priority for him. Therefore he says, "Philosophy is ever thought of as the lamp of all sciences, as the means of all actions (and) as the support of all laws (and duties).[114]

> Control over the senses, which are motivated by the training in the sciences, should be secured by giving up lust, anger, greed, pride, arrogance and overexcitement.[115]

> In the happiness of the subjects lies the benefit of the king and in what is beneficial to the subjects is his own benefit.[116]

He also emphasised that to succeed in public life, one must first succeed in his inner life. Consistently you find the battle is first fought within oneself, to overcome the periodic assaults of negativity afflicted by wrong knowledge and identification.

Like so, the book is filled with insight and the emphasis is clearly on character building or aligning one's personality along spiritual lines. All this eventually makes a person a force for good. The education at Takshashila, combined with Chanakya's counsel, is bound to have built the character of the King. His personality was carefully constructed around certain values and above all it's safe to assume they were grounded in spirituality.

The impact of the King's training

When the king – the man on top, is of such character, it sets the tone in society and the trickle-down effect kicks into play. A good leader inspires, as the Arthashastra affirms:

> If the king is energetic, his subjects will be equally energetic. If he is slack (and lazy in performing his duties) the subjects will also be lazy, thereby, eating into his wealth. Besides, a lazy king will fall into the hands of the enemies. Hence the king himself should always be energetic.[117]

Chandragupta was loved and respected by the people he governed, solely because he was a just and righteous king. After his many conquests he disowned his royal robes, became a monk and thus passed away. His son Bindusarsa continued his legacy. Chanakya remained prime minister even during Bindusara's rule and consolidated the Mauryan Empire.

Character of the average citizen in Mauryan India

Now that we've seen what the leaders were like, let's take a look at the citizens of those times.

Megasthenes wrote:

> The Indians live happily enough, being simple in their manners and frugal. They never drink wine except at sacrifices. Theft is a very rare occurrence. The simplicity of their laws and their contracts is proved by the fact that they seldom go to law court. Their houses and properties they generally leave unguarded. Truth and virtue they hold alike in esteem.[118]

These are the same people that had dominion over an area of three million sq km. So, there must be some power in honesty and simplicity, it certainly seems to have driven the Mauryan Empire to great heights.

Today, a lot of the suffering in society is because of poor and uninspired leadership. One has just to read the Arthashastras to understand the depth and sublimity in Chanakya's thought. His ideas also led to sound decision-making, thereby keeping the country peaceful and prosperous yet alert and ready. One criticism of this era was that punishments were harsh. The Great Ashoka rectified that, and proved that people respond better to love and not fear.

The Great Ashoka

After the Kalinga war, the empire experienced half a century of peace and security under Ashoka. It's no surprise that this period coincided and led to one of India's most prosperous eras economically and socially. The driving force behind this prosperity was the atmosphere of trust and love. He brought *spirituality into governance* – and saw it as the binding force of his kingdom.

The great emperor's character as captured in RC Majumdar's book:

> The emperor not only preached the truths but also practiced them. We read in his records, how, on the roads, he had rest-houses erected, and also caused wells to be dug and trees to be planted, for use of men and beasts.
> "All men are my children," said he, "and just as I desire for my children that they enjoy every kind of prosperity and happiness, in both this world and the next, so also I desire the same for all men.[119]

Ashoka also had a tremendous work ethic, and being the leader, his character and the values he stood for were reflected in society through his reign. Despite his extreme ideals of non-injury, he was an able administrator and maintained prosperity in his large empire.

The Gupta empire

The credit of establishing the Gupta empire largely goes to Samudragupta and his son. Samudragupta was a fierce warrior and a military genius. According to R C Majumdar:

> Samudragupta was really a hero of a hundred fights, as the court poet describes him in a laudatory inscription incised on the Ashokan pillar at Allahabad from which we know all facts about him. He was however, not merely the first soldier of his age, but a statesman of no mean order. He was, besides, a man of culture. The court poet describes him not only as brave and skilful in battle, but also as a patron of learning, a celebrated poet and musician. He was of tolerant spirit, and extended his favour to other religions. This is well illustrated by his gracious donation to the Buddhist king of Ceylon to build a monastery for his subjects at Ceylon.[120]

During this time, scholars such as Kalidasa, Aryabhatta, Varahamihira, Vishnu Sharma and Vatsyayana delivered ground breaking insights. These are relevant even today and their work forms the foundation of many scientific advancements.

The importance of education

Under the patronage of the Gupta empires, the Nalanda and Vikramasila universities and thousands of other educational institutions flourished and nurtured young minds. Nalanda was the most important of them all. It was considered the most influential seat of learning in the world. I can't help but conclude that education in those eras was probably designed and focused on whole brain development.

Here's a description of Nalanda University:

> Nalanda was established in the 5th century AD in Bihar, India. Founded in 427 in north-eastern India, not far from what is today the southern border of Nepal, it survived until 1197. It was devoted to Buddhist studies, but it also trained students in fine arts, medicine, mathematics, astronomy, politics and the art of war.
>
> The centre had eight separate compounds, 10 temples, meditation halls, classrooms, lakes and parks. It had a nine-story library where monks meticulously copied books and documents so that individual scholars could have their own collections. It had dormitories for students, perhaps a first for an educational institution, housing 10,000 students in the university's heyday and providing accommodations for 2,000 professors. Nalanda University attracted pupils and scholars from Korea, Japan, China, Tibet, Indonesia, Persia and Turkey. Hiuen Tsang, the famous pilgrim from China came here and studied and taught for 5 years in the 7th Century A.D. For some 700 years, Nalanda was the centre of knowledge in the world. [121]

Graduates were straight away picked up and given a posting in ministries. *The deserving and qualified alone occupied important positions* and were rightly celebrated and given status. To gain entry into the university, the guards would apparently ask you a question and only if you answered satisfactorily would you be let in.

Hiuen Tsang wrote:

> The day is not sufficient for asking and answering profound questions. From morning till night they engage in profound discussion; the old and the young mutually help one another.[122]

Nalanda had the best of minds. Both students and teachers were of great ability and their names were known in far off lands. Learned men from various cities came to Nalanda to clear their doubts. Writing on the character of men produced by the educational institutions of the day, Hiuen Tsang observed:

> When they have finished their education and have attained thirty years of age, then their character is formed and their knowledge ripe. There are some deeply versed in antiquity, who devote themselves to elegant studies and live apart from the world, and retain the simplicity of their character. These rise above mundane presents and are as insensible towards renown as to the contempt of the world. Their name having spread afar, the rulers appreciate them highly, but are unable to draw them to court.
>
> The chief of the country honours them on account of their gifts, and people exact their fame and render them universal homage. Forgetting fatigue they expatiate in the arts and sciences; seeking for wisdom while "relying on perfect virtue" they count not 150 miles a long journey.[123]

We have heard the observations of Megasthenes of the average Indian in the 3rd century BC. Now let us find out what Hiuen Tsang had to say about the 7th century Indian:

> They are not deceitful or treacherous in their conduct, and are faithful to their oaths and promises. In their rules of government there is remarkable rectitude, whilst in their behaviour there is much gentleness and sweetness.[124]

Thus R C Majumdar concludes, "According to the standards of both the East as well as of the West, Indian character was high and honourable. This was undoubtedly the result of the grand system of education that they had evolved, a system which produced the most comprehensive literature and the best type of men."[125]

To summarise, here are the noteworthy features of this era:

Leadership

- This era produced *great leadership*. The leaders possessed all the necessary skills needed to govern and maintain peace and prosperity.

- There was deep love, understanding and promotion of spirituality and culture. The leadership propagated core religious values in society through their actions. They were primary *driving forces* that led to prosperity.
- Leadership showed a great *balance between head and heart.* Their hearts and minds were soft for the needs of the people and their might strong against enemies of the state.
- They themselves were brilliant and were surrounded by luminous minds.
- They were loved by their citizens.

Education

- India was considered to be the most influential seat of learning.
- The *education* imparted was *spiritually grounded,* and aided all-round development of the brain. Students developed intelligence emotionally, morally, cognitively, spiritually and socially (in contrast, today's education is commerce centric.)
- The focus of all education was *character building.*

Role models

- Great *sages, poets and teachers* emerged and were revered, respected and afforded the highest status and positions in society.
- The top echelons of society were occupied by minds possessed with noble ideas. As a result, young minds had *great role models* and teachers to emulate. Their thoughts and works pervaded society's consciousness.
- Expertise in society – scholarly work advanced various fields of *science, arts, culture, politics, warfare and religion* as mentioned earlier.

Results

We were the richest country in the world both spiritually and materially.

Returning to the present and cricket, ever since the NCA (National Cricket Academy) was set up in Bengaluru, Indian cricket has produced better results. Scholars, mentors and teachers of all disciplines reside there. They also travel around the country disseminating state of the art cricketing knowledge, thereby flooding the system with coaches par excellence. This will go a long way in securing the cricketing future of the country. I hope this institution continues to flourish.

We are successors of a rich spiritual mind. For instance, when a sport or activity relies more on mental powers as opposed to physical skills you find that Indians excel. The world champion in chess for a long time belonged to our country. The bulk of our medals in the recent past in the Olympics have come from shooting. With the change in surfaces and rules that made the game of hockey more physical, we find ourselves missing out on medals. Cricket too is more mental than physical, and once we improved our physical side we became world-beaters.

The point of this is to recognise the inherent character, intelligence and energy of this nation and use it to benefit you. The British historian E P Thompson once said, "There is not a thought that is being thought in the West or East that is not active in some Indian mind."[126] There is no doubt we have the mind.

Perhaps what we need is to improve on our weaknesses gradually, but never at the cost of our strengths. This leads to a balance between the best of the West and the best of the East, a balance between materialism and spirituality.

Indian society has been through a metamorphosis and over time the idealism has been beaten out of it by repeated assaults. In keeping noble ideas flexible and relevant to the changing times without diluting their essence, society needed genuinely selfless and spiritual people. Unfortunately, over time a majority of the lofty principles were poorly executed and hence discredited.

However, history has come a full circle. For if it was the *compassion of Prithviraj Chauhan* that first led to foreign rule, it was *compassion again employed by Mahatma Gandhi* that won us back our freedom.

Spirituality is the exercise that unleashes human will and when set free, the resulting wave of energy will sweep the obstacles that stand in the way of your path. Further, your endeavour will most likely aid society at large.

The values institutionalised today are designed not to liberate the mind, but to enslave it to propaganda. Can we bring back what is needed? 'Be the change you wish to see in the world' the Father of our nation said, too idealistic a notion some may think. But it is up to us – society's trustees, its value and culture creators to forge a better future. The power is in our hands, drop-by-drop, tear-by-tear, ball-by-ball, match-by-match. In our own small way, can we not work to restore truth?

Endnotes

1 Martin Crowe, *How McCullum helped me let go*, ESPNCricinfo, 18 February 2014. http://www.espncricinfo.com/magazine/content/story/720283.html

2 Ibid

3 Ibid

4 Quoted in: Mukund Padmanabhan, *One Man's Ooty*, The Hindu, 16 January 2005 http://hindu.com/thehindu/mag/2005/01/16/stories/2005011600580100.htm

5 Interview in the Scientific American, 1 July 2008 http://www.scientificamerican.com/article/the-mirror-neuron-revolut/

6 Mr Irfan Sait is someone who takes great pains in running KIOC. Like BPCA, over the years KIOC too has made high performance cricket knowledge available locally. He regularly invites cricket related as well as experts of various persuasions to chat with trainees, providing both insight and motivation. BPCA and KIOC are always abuzz with cricketing life.

7 Jawahar's Cricket Academy under Mr Prashanth's guidance too has got an excellent cricket culture going. Bengaluru has been blessed with an abundance of these institutions.

8 The Dalai Lama website, 28 November 2012 http://www.dalailama.com/news/post/885-at-tumkur-university-his-holiness-the-dalai-lama-inaugurates-a-conference-about-yoga-in-education-and-later-meets-with-Bengaluru-based-tibetans

9 *Jeremy Hunt highlights plight of 'chronically lonely'*, BBC news, 18 October 2013 http://www.bbc.com/news/uk-politics-24572231

10 *I am a Voice without a Form,* Vivekananda Institute of Human Excellence, p11

11 Mr Arun Shourie is also a former cabinet minister, journalist, economist and the author of several books.

12 Palkhivala Foundation Lecture http://www.youtube.com/watch?v=VIIUjdswN0I

13 The movie 'Invictus' is a must watch. It's about how Nelson Mandela inspired the South African rugby team to a World Cup victory.

14 Diwan of the princely state of Mysore.

15 These are all India tournaments played by top teams and players in the country, and hosted in Chennai and Hyderabad respectively.

16 Maharashtra has three cricket teams – Mumbai, Maharashtra and Vidarbha.

17 Gujarat has three cricket teams – Gujarat, Baroda and Saurashtra.

18 Jawahars, Swastik Union and BUCC.

19 Greg Baum, *Cricketers break the silence on problem of depression that has struck down so many*, The Age, 27 November 2013. http://m.theage.com.au/sport/cricket/cricketers-break-the-silence-on-problem-of-depression-that-has-struck-down-so-many-20131126-2y87d.html

20 David Frith, *Hit wicket: Why do cricketers commit suicide?*, DNA, 19 November 2011. http://www.dnaindia.com/sport/column-hit-wicket-why-do-cricketers-commit-suicide-1614619

21 Dr Suratwala was Head of Sports Science in The National Cricket Academy (NCA) and also a much sought after mental toughness expert.

22 Former India and Karnataka player.

23 Mr Makarand arrived in Karnataka as a TRDO (Talent Resource Development Officer) and consultant. He is also a journalist whose bold articles routinely appear in leading newspapers in the country. He was instrumental in introducing me to both D Y Patil and Mumbai.

24 Coach, mentor, teacher, guide and tutor are all different words used to describe an educator. Parents too are our first educators.

25 J. Krishnamurti, *Letters to the Schools, Volume 2,* 15 November 1982 http://www.jkrishnamurti.org/krishnamurti-teachings/view-text.php?tid=40&chid=329

26 My family affectionately refers to him as Shankar Swami; he has been a family mentor and cricket guide for my brother, my father and myself. He is venerated in Kodagu and besides cricket also coaches those interested in hockey and golf.

27 Former Karnataka Ranji Trophy player and Goa coach, with Level 3 NCA coaching accreditation.

28 Karnataka won the Ranji Trophy, Irani Cup and Vijay Hazare Trophy

29 http://www.peepalgroveschool.org/

30 Sachin Tendulkar's First Press Conference Post Retirement, 18 Niovember 2013 http://www.youtube.com/watch?v=JKIeOGxAjYs

31 Ex Goa Ranji trophy player. He also got 170 in that game.

32 http://www.goodreads.com/quotes/101458-everybody-is-a-genius-but-if-you-judge-a-fish

33 Radhakrishnan Pillai, *Corporate Chanakya*, (Jaico)

34 Sachin Tendulkar's First Press Conference Post Retirement, 18 November 2013 Lhttp://www.youtube.com/watch?v=JKIeOGxAjYs – between the 35 and 40th minutes.

35 Oxford dictionaries http://www.oxforddictionaries.com/definition/english/pneumonoultramicroscopicsilicovolcanoconiosis

36 J. Krishnamurti, *On Education* http://www.jkrishnamurti.com/krishnamurti-teachings/view-text.php?tid=43&chid=297

37 TED talk, February 2004 https://www.ted.com/talks/mihaly_csikszentmihalyi_on_flow/transcript?language=en#t-919000 (transcript)

38 Eben Novy-Williams, *Lance Armstrong says he cheated, lied, bullied during career,* Bloomberg, 19 January 2013 http://www.bloomberg.com/news/2013-01-18/lance-armstrong-says-he-cheated-lied-bullied-throughout-career.html

39 Ex – Karnataka opening batsman and South Zone.

40 A breathing technique that is meant to calm the mind by focusing on one's breath.

41 http://rescomp.stanford.edu/~cheshire/EinsteinQuotes.html

42 An entrepreneur, he is also an avid golfer and very active in the amateur circuit. He is a keen student of psychology.

43 For more information about Sri M, visit the Satsang Foundation website http://satsang-foundation.org/

44 Sri M, *The Jewel in the Lotus*, Magenta Press

45 This idea was popularized by the writer Malcolm Gladwell in his book, Outliers (2008).

46 Ruzbeh N Bharucha, *The Fakir*, Full Circle (2010), p243.

47 Abraham Harold Maslow was an American psychologist famous for Maslow's pyramid that details the hierarchy of human needs.

48 Jill Bolte Taylor, *My Stroke of Insight*, Hodder Publishers, p15

49 http://www.goodreads.com/quotes/424657-we-are-not-physical-beings-having-a-spiritual-experience-we

50 Owen Gibson, *The hidden crisis of mental health among footballers*, The Guardian, 5 August 2013 http://www.theguardian.com/football/2013/aug/05/mental-health-footballers-alcoholism-retirement

51 The complete works of Swami Vivekananda, Volume 1, p80

52 Words of Sri M

53 Shri M, *Jewel in the lotus,* Magenta Press, p22

54 Ibid p22-23

55 Ibid p5

56 Ibid p42

57 Ibid p40

58 Shloka 5 of the Ishavasya Upanishad.

59 This is the same method that I tweaked a little and used against Western Railway to make an unbeaten 113 in the Times Shield. You will find a detailed account of it in the chapter on Goalkeeping.

60 Technically, only the present is real. Almost all thoughts take you to either the future or the past, which do not physically exist at any given point.

61 Counter thinking is not a new technique. The reason the technique worked for me is that the counters were all based on fact, and my mind had fully grasped this.

62 Swami Vivekananda on Himself, *Vivekananda Biography*, p313, www.advaithaashrama.org

63 http://zapatopi.net/kelvin/quotes/

64 Steve Connor, *Belief and the brain's 'God spot',* The Independent, 10 March 2009. http://www.independent.co.uk/news/science/belief-and-the-brains-god-spot-1641022.html

65 https://www.coursera.org/course/bluebrain

66 http://hyperphysics.phy-astr.gsu.edu/nave-html/faithpathh/crick.html

67 A sophisticated link mechanism that passes information from one neuron to another locally, and sometimes to different regions of the brain. There are billions of such neurons, axons, synapses and their connections.

68 http://curiosity.discovery.com/question/blue-brain-project Blue Brain Project website http://bluebrain.epfl.ch/

69 American Institute of Physics http://www.aip.org/history/einstein/voice1.htm

70 Jeff Lieberman http://bea.st/inevolution/?p=264

71 Jeff Lieberman http://bea.st/inevolution/?m=201203

72 The complete works of Swami Vivekananda, Volume 7/Conversations and dialogues/VI http://en.wikisource.org/wiki/The_Complete_Works_of_Swami_Vivekananda/Volume_7/Conversations_And_Dialogues/VI

73 Jeff Lieberman http://bea.st/inevolution/?p=264

74 Sri M, *Apprenticed to a Himalayan Master*, Magenta Press

75 There are other classifications or perspectives to the brain. I am simply using Dr Taylor's words to explain her stroke.

76 A band of nerve fibres that connects and aids in communication between the left and right hemispheres of the brain. It transfers motor, sensory and cognitive information between the two sides.

77 Jill Bolte Taylor, TED talk https://www.youtube.com/watch?v=UyyjU8fzEYU, transcript available at http://www.ted.com/talks/jill_bolte_taylor_s_powerful_stroke_of_insight/ transcript?language=en#t-246000

78 Ibid

79 Ibid

80 Ibid

81 Ibid

82 Information flows from one neuron to another neuron across a synapse.

83 TEDx talk http://www.youtube.com/watch?v=m8rRzTtP7Tc

84 The amygdala is the fight or flight part of the reptilian brain.

85 Though I am relating a 'B' division game, I used the same mental approach to score a century against BPCL in the Times 'A' division a couple of seasons later.

86 Albert Einstein official site http://einstein.biz/quotes.php

87 Michael Mauboussin, *The Paradox of Skill*, ChangeThis http://changethis.com/manifesto/100.03.SuccessEquation/pdf/100.03.SuccessEquation.pdf

88 Ibid

89 Ibid

90 http://bleacherreport.com/articles/910238-the-100-best-sports-quotes-of-all-time/page/18

91 *Chappell's Notorious Underarm Delivery* – you can watch the incident on YouTube: http://www.youtube.com/watch?v=UkQRERykq5M

92 Martin Williamson, *Underhand, Underam,* ESPNCricinfo, 21 January 2011http://www.espncricinfo.com/magazine/content/story/498574.html

93 The Telegraph, 1 August 2011 http://www.telegraph.co.uk/sport/cricket/international/india/8674845/England-v-India-Anil-Kumble-and-Gundappa-Viswanath-praise-MS-Dhonis-gesture-to-Ian-Bell.html

94 http://bleacherreport.com/articles/910238-the-100-best-sports-quotes-of-all-time/page/18 -

95 http://www.theguardian.com/sport/gallery/2011/jul/03/wimbledon-novak-djokovic-rafael-nadal

96 http://bleacherreport.com/articles/910238-the-100-best-sports-quotes-of-all-time/page/18

97 *Owens' Legacy: a National Icon*, Ohio State University http://library.osu.edu/projects/jesse-owens/story_legacy.html

98 David James, *Rafael Nadal says he owes French Open success to fear of failure*, AFP, 11 June 2011. http://sports.nationalpost.com/2012/06/11/rafael-nadal-says-he-owes-french-open-success-to-fear-of-failure/

99 Madhur Tankha, *Fear of failure makes me work hard, says Shah Rukh Khan,* The Hindu, 27 September 2013 http://www.thehindu.com/todays-paper/tp-national/tp-newdelhi/fear-of-failure-makes-me-work-hard-says-shah-rukh-khan/article5173509.ece

100 http://www.henryfordquotes.org/one-who-fears-failure-limits-his-activities-failure-is-only-the-opportunity-to-more-intelligently-begin-again/

101 http://www.brainyquote.com/quotes/quotes/n/napoleonbo116693.html

102 http://www.brainyquote.com/quotes/quotes/t/thomasaed132683.html

103 Eric Zorn, *Without failure, Jordan would be a false idol,* Chicago Tribune, 19 May 1997 http://articles.chicagotribune.com/1997-05-19/news/9705190096_1_nike-mere-rumor-driver-s-license

104 http://www.zdnet.com/in-his-own-words-bill-gates-best-quotes-3040151687/

105 Mark Shnurman, *Breaking the four minute mile,* Commercial Observer http://commercialobserver.com/2014/05/breaking-the-four-minute-mile/

106 http://womenshistory.about.com/od/quotes/a/joyner_kersee.htm

107 Malcolm Gladwell, *Complexity and the ten thousand hour rule,* The New Yorker, 2013 http://www.newyorker.com/news/sporting-scene/complexity-and-the-ten-thousand-hour-rule

108 Interview with Steve Jobs http://www.youtube.com/watch?v=ZWaX1g_2SSQ

109 https://www.goodreads.com/author/quotes/17287.Shashi_Tharoor

110 Quoted in Sri Paramahansa Yogananda's *Autobiography of a Yogi*, p232.

111 Quoted in R C Majumdar's *Ancient India*, Motilal Banarsidass, 1977, p219

112 Ibid p108

113 Radhakrishnan Pillai, *Corporate Chanakya*, Jaico, p24

114 Ibid p36

115 Ibid p8

116 Ibid p168

117 Ibid p14

118 Ancient India as described by Megasthenes and Arrian, Google Play (free ebook), p69-70

119 R C Majumdar, *Ancient India*, Motilal Banarsidass,1977, p108 -114

120 Ibid p232-233

121 All India Council for Technical Education http://www.aicte-india.org/downloads/ancient.pdf

122 R C Majumdar, *Ancient India*, Motilal Banarsidass,1977, p453

123 Ibid p454

124 Ibid

125 Ibid

126 Quoted in: Shashi Tharoor, *So Long, Farewell*, 2008. http://www.shashitharoor.in/the-hindu-column-details.php?id=16

Closing thoughts

About eight years ago, I was introduced to a 20-year-old cricketer who was willing to go the extra mile in order to achieve his goal of playing cricket at the highest level for India. The passion in his eyes was unmistakable.

He had taken the courageous step of leaving his comfortable home and family in Bengaluru in order to pursue his dreams. Most Bangaloreans I know loathe leaving the city known for its salubrious climate all year round but Ashwath took the risk of venturing out to Mumbai to try his fortunes in the tougher local leagues, living out of a small rented room in Airoli, Navi Mumbai.

The efforts being put in by this lad were commendable – hours of training in the gym coupled with dedicated practice sessions on the field took up most of his day. But the results that he got in competition did not often reflect the methodical preparation that he was putting in, as it so often happens to many young sportsmen.

He was open to all ideas and suggestions on improving his performance and that's when we started having meaningful discussions on developing the mental side of his game. The results were good, but not consistent enough. Soon I began to perceive some frustration creeping into him. I could see that he had forgotten the primary motive of why he started playing cricket in the first place – i.e. to enjoy the game. All too often, a morose Ashwath would have to be reminded to enjoy the process and await a favourable outcome.

His journey after that is well chronicled in this excellent book. When the spiritual dimension of his game and life were opened up to him by his mentors, it resulted in Ashwath finally discovering and accepting the true champion within himself.

The book is a result of in-depth research combined with sharing of personal experiences, which will be of enormous help to many budding youngsters who put in hours of toil. These youngsters can take a leaf out of Ashwath's journey and find their true selves through enjoying and embracing their sport. It will also be a valuable companion to those who do make it 'big' in understanding and appreciating the spiritual dimension of sport.

Fearlessly written, the message of this book fulfils a burning need that for too long has been unaddressed. Finally, it will be a fantastic guide to sports parents, coaches and others connected with developing sportsmen to realise that every kid can be a champion in life, irrespective of what scorecards and bank balances say.

– Dr. Kinjal Suratwala

At the time of writing Head of Sports Science and Coach Education, National Cricket Academy (NCA), Bengaluru

About the author

For the past two years Ashwath Aiyappa worked extremely hard on writing this book, completing the manuscript before his untimely demise in tragic circumstances.

Ashwath began playing cricket at a very young age, and found early success when he represented the Karnataka state Under-16 team. He was also a Ranji probable and played first division league cricket for several top clubs in Bengaluru and Mumbai – Jawahars, Swastik Union, BUCC and DY Patil. In addition, he undertook coaching assignments at the Peepal Grove School in Sadum (Andhra Pradesh), where he was much loved and adored by the children.

With a degree in computer science from St Joseph's College, Ashwath continued being a student throughout. He had a huge appetite for knowledge – he read widely on a range of subjects including psychology, philosophy, religion, history, business and of course sport. Ashwath also undertook several online training courses and sought the advice of various experts. Apart from his sporting achievements, he was an entrepreneur. He co-founded a very successful software company, later selling his stake to concentrate on cricket.

It is not easy to write a book. This is particularly true for anyone who is more accustomed to spending long hours on the playing field with teammates, rather than months alone in front of a computer. Yet, Ashwath was supremely determined because above all else, he wished to help youngsters. He wanted them to be better equipped to deal with the trials and tribulations of a sporting career. So he taught himself the skills required to write a book and put in enormous effort, the result of which is in your hands.

Ashwath had a burning desire to bring spirituality into all those associated with sport including administrators, players, coaches, trainers and sponsors. This would enable them to become not just better professionals, but better human beings. Spirituality is not ordinarily linked to sport though hopefully this book will begin the process of change.

Ashwath was a hero in every sense of the word. He lived in accordance with the highest principles and was an inspiration to all around him. He stole the hearts of everyone his life touched, across generations – children, grown-ups and the elderly. He wore his wisdom lightly and injected humour, fun and joy into the lives of people. His loss is truly irreplaceable. We pray that his soul rests in peace.

To stay in touch with Ashwath's legacy, please visit ashwathaiyappa.com.

A note from the author's parents

Our sons were our lives. Our world revolved around them. Dr Akhil Kuttappa and Ashwath Aiyappa were wonderful children – they were loving, hardworking, caring, responsible, and God-loving. They were also charming, articulate and athletic. Above all, they were good human beings who found happiness in helping other people.

Life was beautiful until cruel fate snatched them both in a tragic accident in April 2014. Ashwath showed his divine quality by sacrificing his life trying to save his brother. People say time is a great healer, but the dastardly act of fate will make sure that we carry the agony of losing our exceptional children till the end of our lives.

Akhil obtained a Master's degree in Periodontology and Implants and was a certified Clinical Endodontist. He taught at the Vydehi Institute of Dental Sciences and Research Centre (Bengaluru), and also ran a successful dental clinic of his own. We are moved to tears as we re-read this heartfelt tribute paid by his Principal, colleagues and students at the Institute:

> Your son and our dear colleague Dr Akhil Kuttappa was a very proactive, hardworking individual with a positive outlook towards life. He had a very fresh innovative approach to clinical dentistry and has contributed immensely in developing clinical skills for both post-graduate and undergraduate students. He was loved and popular among the students, always had a smile on his face and was ever ready to lend a helping hand. More importantly, he was a noble person who will be missed not just by our department, but by the entire college. His demise has left a deep void in our personal and professional lives which is impossible to be filled by anybody.

Ashwath, who we lovingly called Baba, had a radiant smile and a warm heart. Though passionate about his cricket all along, he never neglected his studies or his work. He co-founded a successful web solutions company called Myndsets Technologies at a young age.

Now, we can also say that he is a debutant author who wanted to build a career based on his strongly held beliefs, which are all in the book. Unfortunately as fate would have it, he didn't live to see his book launch for which he had put his heart and soul into. The book was to be released in May 2014, but God bowled us a googly. We are sure you will find the book interesting, insightful, and useful. We are proud of our sons' achievements. We will miss and love them always. May their great souls rest in great peace.

– Anitha and Raghu Madappa

Praise for the book

Peak performance states or the 'zone' in sports occur when the mind is free of distraction and totally absorbed in action. As such sport has the power to produce spiritual states of mind. To say it plainly, spirituality too is a gradual process towards becoming established in the present. In simple language, Ashwath has explained how he practically applied spirituality to better his life. This book is for everyone, not just sportspeople, and my blessings are with it.

– ***Sri M***

This book is simply brilliant. It talks about how 'failure' can teach you (if you let it). Ashwath was a dedicated cricketer and a decade ago he changed the definition of hard work. Sadly, dedication doesn't always guarantee success, but ultimately the only real failure in life is not knowing how to be happy. With beautiful narration he presents an alternate vantage point, and explains how in the end cricket gave him more than he could have ever asked for.

– ***Makarand Waingankar***
Senior Journalist (contributes to The Hindu and Times of India). He is a cricket management consultant and launched the TRDO -Talent Resource Development project for BCCI.

Cricket is not only about skill level and temperament but it's also about luck, no matter how hard you work. Lakhs of players play, thousands work hard but only 11 can play in a team. Ashwath was a talented and hardworking cricketer and this book is a result of his intense experience. It introduces a dimension seldom spoken of, and ends up being a book not merely about cricket, but about life. Very interesting and absorbing, it is a must for sportspeople and for those associated with sport.

– ***Brijesh Patel***
Former India Test Player and Secretary of the Karnataka State Cricket Association

Ashwath speaks from authentic personal experience and provides a spiritual perspective tailor-made for young sportspeople. They will know that googlies are bowled all the time and in various forms. This book offers you a way of playing them successfully.

– ***Sujith Somasundar***

Ex India Cricketer, Life Coach and Mental Conditioning expert